Charles Ringma has taught in universities, colleges and seminaries in Asia, Australia and Canada. He is Professor Emeritus at Regent College, Vancouver, a Franciscan Tertiary and a Companion of the Northumbria Community, Brisbane. He has written many books on Christian spirituality, including *Hear the Ancient Wisdom* (SPCK, 2013). See <faithcompanions.com>.

Mary Dickau has been on the pastoral leadership team of Grandview Calvary Baptist Church, Vancouver, for 25 years. She is a spiritual director and hosts a city retreat called Stillpointe, facilitating weekly rhythms of prayer and times of healing prayer.

T0341931

'A truly remarkable achievement, *The Art of Healing Prayer* is a book like no other in its subject matter, taking the meaning of "comprehensive" to new levels. I am astonished at how such a concise book can be so wide-ranging and yet so complete!

'It is at once creative and reflective, theological and practical, knowledgeable and flexible, and deeply spiritual. The authors offer guidelines and examples as they lead us through a case-study format involving preparation prayers and practical healing prayers, as well as pastoral follow-up prayers, ideally for a participatory team. The suggested examples of healing prayers used throughout the book are quite profound and powerfully appropriate.

'Based on [the authors'] decades of hands-on experience in training both clergy and laity, *The Art of Healing Prayer* has authenticity, understanding and wisdom oozing from its pages. Here is no triumphalist theorizing but recognition that to seek God's heart for healing on behalf of others is not a quick fix; rather, it requires an awareness that the inner, outer and relational healing of the whole person – body, mind and spirit – involves an on-going healing journey.

'The authors are to be commended: I believe this book, although relatively slim, will prove to be a huge gift to the whole faith community.'

The Revd Trevor Miller, Abbot of the
Northumbria Community

'Living closely with those who've been marginalized, I have witnessed how inner wounds plague people for life. And I have seen how their wounds – often more visible because of their vulnerability – expose the wounds of others. How does the Spirit work in this brokenness? Charles and Mary have given us a practical guide and liturgical resource for healing prayer. I know it's good news because reading it has helped me see better how the Spirit is at work where I live.'

Jonathan Wilson-Hartgrove, author of
Common Prayer *and* Strangers at My Door

THE ART OF HEALING PRAYER

Bringing Christ's wholeness to broken people

Charles Ringma
and
Mary Dickau

First published in Great Britain in 2015

Society for Promoting Christian Knowledge
36 Causton Street
London SW1P 4ST
www.spck.org.uk

The authors and publisher have made every effort to ensure that the external website
and email addresses included in this book are correct and up to date at the time of
going to press. The authors and publisher are not responsible for the content,
quality or continuing accessibility of the sites.

Scripture quotations are from the New Revised Standard Version of the Bible,
Anglicized Edition, copyright © 1989, 1995 by the Division of Christian
Education of the National Council of the Churches of Christ in
the USA. Used by permission. All rights reserved.

The publisher and authors acknowledge with thanks permission to reproduce
extracts from the following:
on p. viii, 'Come Healing', from *Old Ideas* by Leonard Cohen;
on p. 129, 'Underneath the Shadow of Your Wings'. Words and Music by Tom Wuest.
Copyright © 2010 Brass Trumpet Publishing. All rights reserved.

British Library Cataloguing-in-Publication Data
A catalogue record for this book is available from the British Library

ISBN 978–0–281–06083–2
eBook ISBN 978–0–281–07567–6

Typeset by Graphicraft Limited, Hong Kong
First printed in Great Britain by Ashford Colour Press
Subsequently digitally printed in Great Britain

eBook by Graphicraft Limited, Hong Kong

Produced on paper from sustainable forests

Contents

Preface   ix

Introduction   xiii

 1 Dimensions of the healing ministry   1

 2 A case study   18

 3 Preparation prayers   24

 4 Inner healing: opening prayers   36

 5 Listening time: prayers of discernment   48

 6 Prayers of confession and repentance   55

 7 Prayers of forgiveness   67

 8 Prayers of separation   80

 9 Prayers for deliverance   92

10 Prayers of inner healing   106

11 Prayers for the infilling of the Holy Spirit   121

12 Prayers of protection and closure   128

13 Follow-up and conclusion   136

Notes   143

Bibliography   149

Come Healing

O gather up the brokenness
And bring it to me now
The fragrance of those promises
You never dared to vow.

The splinters that you carry
The cross you left behind
Come healing of the body
Come healing of the mind . . .

O solitude of longing
Where love has been confined
Come healing of the body
Come healing of the mind.

O see the darkness yielding
That tore the light apart
Come healing of the reason
Come healing of the heart . . .

O let the heavens falter
And let the earth proclaim:
Come healing of the altar
Come healing of the Name.

And let the heavens hear it
The penitential hymn
Come healing of the spirit
Come healing of the limb.

(Leonard Cohen in *Old Ideas*)

Preface

The particular focus of this book about inner healing is to assist both clergy and laity in developing greater understanding and skills when praying for those who are seeking the healing of Christ. Thus this book emphasizes how to pray biblically, imaginatively and sensitively for those who are seeking help in their journey towards wholeness.

The book assumes that the reader has an understanding of the healing ministry of Christ in the world through the Church and also that the reader may already be exercising a ministry of prayer. Thus the theological and biblical bases for the healing ministry in the life of the Church are largely assumed. But they are briefly touched upon in the opening chapter and throughout the book whenever it is necessary to provide a framework and setting for healing prayers. Though the case for Christian healing will not be systematically developed, that may be the topic for another book, since there has been little theological reflection about healing in much of the contemporary literature on this topic. This book seeks to fill a gap in the books that have already been written about healing prayer, as most contain few actual examples of prayers for healing.[1]

In the communal and internal life of the Church, worship, teaching and Eucharist typically hold central place, with the ministry of healing as a poor second cousin to all that the Church seeks to offer. Furthermore, because healing has largely been outsourced to the medical profession and psychologists, most churches do not include prayers for healing as part of the normal pastoral ministry of the Church. As a result, many clergy and laity do not know how to do this well.

Moreover, in the Western Church in particular, we do not tend to cultivate a faithful or vibrant life of prayer anyway – let alone praying for healing and deliverance.

The Church has often become a very functional and pragmatic institution. We provide social services rather than tend the ministries of contemplation and prayer. We conduct religious services that build people up for practical service and well-being rather than develop them for a life of sacrifice, prayer and spiritual discernment.

೮೨೮೩

This book has its roots in my 30-year journey of participating in training clergy and laity for establishing healing teams in churches and para-church organizations in both the minority world (the West) and majority world settings. It has also emerged from training theological students to make healing prayers part of their future pastoral ministry. We are particularly grateful to the many students who, over the past 16 years or so, have participated in inner-healing seminars, both at the Asian Theological Seminary in Manila, Philippines, and at Regent College in Vancouver, Canada. These participants not only theologically and intellectually opened their hearts and minds to the healing ministry, but some also sought healing prayers for their own lives. For their openness and vulnerability, we are deeply grateful. This book is dedicated to these students, who have carried this ministry into many parts of the globe.

We have used the word 'art' in the title of this book to convey that healing prayers are a creative activity. While there are careful strategies and skilful practices in healing prayer, there is also much room for imagination, creativity and flexibility. The movement of prayer is multidirectional, for as we respond to a particular person and his or her story and needs, we are also open to the mysterious but accompanying workings of the Spirit, while at the same time we bring our own skills, sensitivities and discernment into the prayer setting. When we engage in prayers for healing, we join with the Lord of the dance. Yet good theology must still guide us and structure our prayers.

Several people have contributed to this book by serving and praying for students in both schools: Dr Athena Gorospe and

Dr Amanda Tan at the Asian Theological Seminary, and Mr Mike Wallbridge and the Revd Sarah Tillett at Regent College. I also wish to acknowledge my indebtedness to Anne White, with whom I trained in schools that prepared clergy and laity to bring the inner-healing ministry into churches in Australia. And I am deeply thankful to my wife, Rita, and friends in Brisbane who over many years regularly prayed for those seeking inner healing.

But special thanks go to Mary Dickau, my teaching assistant at Regent College, who has not only been a great help in running the inner-healing seminars and helping to pray for people seeking help, but who has been inspirational in opening up new ways of prayer. I am also grateful for her participation in the writing of this book. Throughout this book, her voice of prayer, longing and hope will be displayed in a different font, guiding you as you pray for those seeking Christ's healing presence in their lives.

Prayer is, at its very core, the witness of death becoming life. This means that the art of healing prayer is, at least in part, the art of dying to self. We become less, so that Christ can become more within us and in our prayers for another. This sacrificial aspect of praying for others makes our prayers safe, so that the journey towards healing and wholeness is marked by hope and goodness for those whose story we are holding before God. In this way, our prayers become sacraments of God's healing, comfort and provision, which flow from the death and resurrection of Jesus. Thus prayer marks the continuing surprise of the abundant life we have in Christ, even in the midst of a broken and pain-filled world. By God's Spirit, our prayers lead us into safe places of shelter and rest as we journey towards our eternal home in God.

Finally, a special thanks to Pieter Kwant of Piquant Agency for placing this book with SPCK and for the good editorial work of our friend and fellow traveller Karen Hollenbeck-Wuest.

Charles Ringma and Mary Dickau
Brisbane, Australia, and
Vancouver, Canada

Introduction

This book invites readers to enter the wide spaces of God's restorative love and forgiveness in Christ through the Spirit to bring healing, comfort and wholeness to the world. This ministry of healing is first and foremost a prayer ministry – not a ministry of demand, but rather of expectation. In healing prayer, we ask God in Christ through the Spirit to come with healing grace and power to the person seeking help. Our prayer posture is neither begging nor triumphalistic. Rather, we pray with a faith, love and hope that is rooted in the nature of who God is and in the promises of the biblical story. Thus this ministry is not about what we humans do, although we do play a role in God's healing activity. Some describe our role as being channels of God's love and healing, yet it is possibly better to describe our role as being assistants to the Holy Spirit. Or, to use a different analogy, we seek to discern what God is doing in bringing healing to a particular person, and we pray for and agree with God's gracious activity. This emphasizes that our prayers are not the source of healing, but rather God's presence, through the Spirit, is the source of all healing. Prayer, then, becomes an act of solidarity with God's action among us, rather than wringing from God's seeming reluctant hand what is difficult to attain. Thus presence rather than demand is the gestalt of all healing prayers.

The ministry of inner healing is part of Christ's spacious healing ministry. In joining this ministry, we pray that Christ's healing and restorative presence, through the brooding Holy Spirit, will bring healing and wholeness to the wounded and broken places within us. Our woundedness can be the result of other people's sins against us, our sinning against ourselves, and the brokenness that comes as a result of living in a fallen world and participating in institutions that, though marked by God's common grace, are also characterized by sin and dysfunction. Thus we can be deeply wounded by living in a negative and broken family or being part of an unhealthy and oppressive social institution. But we can also be wounded by making poor choices that lead to wrongdoing – thereby sinning against ourselves. Thus the inner-healing ministry includes prayers for forgiveness, absolution, deliverance, healing, restoration and infilling as we ask God to bring wholeness to people, rather than merely relief from particular problems.

To say that healing is primarily a prayer ministry does not suggest that other factors do not contribute to the healing process. The healing ministry of the Church recognizes many other dimensions in the healing process, including the use of symbolism and sacramentalism. Thus Scripture, praise, the Eucharist, the laying on of hands and anointing with oil all play a role in the ministry of inner healing. But the basic frame supporting all of these remains prayer, for in prayer we humbly come before God to seek grace and help.

In providing a framework for inner healing, we will outline a variety of prayers that can be appropriated by the reader. These prayers are not normative, but rather suggestive. They are designed as signposts rather than as models, and our concern is not so much with methods as inspiration. For no particular prayer can have universal validity, because as unique people, we pray for others out of our understandings of their settings, personalities, backgrounds and issues. Thus our prayers must always be specific and contextual, as well as intuitive, reflective and creative – and each of us will need to find our own voice as we pray healing prayers.

Though the prayers set out in this book are primarily spoken, we do not believe in 'word magic', where we just speak something out and it will be done, or where we claim something aloud and it shall come to pass. Instead, we believe in the performative nature of prayer spoken in faith, hope and love in resonance with God's will and purpose. We believe in the Spirit accompanying the word, but also in the sovereign freedom of the Spirit. And as we humbly draw near to God through our prayers, we connect the divine with the human.

ဆၢၓ

To guide readers through this book, Chapter 1 will set out basic perspectives regarding the broader healing ministry of the community of faith and then identify the place of inner healing within that framework. Chapter 2 describes a case study that will provide the focus for the ministry of inner healing. The rest of the book is divided up into three major sections: preparation prayers, healing prayers and pastoral follow-up prayers. Within each of these sections, we will explore important subtopics.

In the section on preparation prayers (Chapter 3), we will provide a set of guidelines for preparing a person for healing prayers and will offer examples of prayers for both the counsellee and the counsellor. We will also explore the importance of discerning prayers (Chapter 5), which involve a careful reflective process about the kind of prayer intervention or other forms of help that may be the most appropriate for the counsellee. Preparation prayers also have to do with the matter of timing. For example, we discern if the person needs more time to be attentive to the Holy Spirit before proceeding to healing prayers. In such a case, we would guide the person seeking healing towards deeper self-reflection, rather than moving directly to getting help and relief.

In the healing prayer section, we will explore many forms and dimensions of prayer, including opening prayers (Chapter 4) and closing prayers (Chapter 12) for the prayer ministry time. We will also discuss prayers of repentance (Chapter 6), forgiveness and absolution (Chapter 7), separation (Chapter 8) and deliverance (Chapter 9), as well as the art of healing prayers (Chapter 10), prayers for the infilling of the Holy Spirit (Chapter 11) and prayers of protection and closure (Chapter 12). While this section focuses specifically on the prayer ministry time, it is important to remember that prayer is central to the whole healing process – the preparation, the healing itself and the follow-up. In the ministry of inner-healing prayer, things are not done to and for a *passive* recipient. Rather, the journey is participatory, and the person seeking healing is invited to pray throughout every phase of the whole process.

The purpose of follow-up prayers (Chapter 13) is to encourage and empower those who are seeking healing to continue to pray as they go forward along the journey towards wholeness. At the same time, the counsellors discern if further pastoral care is needed.

As we companion others along this costly journey towards wholeness, we will need to open our own lives to the gift of God's healing grace so that we can become available to those seeking restoration. And as others are transformed by God's healing grace in their lives, they often are empowered to pray for healing for others in the future. In this way, the beauty and goodness of God's grace extends further into the world through ever-expanding ripples of new life, hope and transformation.

ℰℭ

Holy One,

you have made your peace with the world. Through Jesus Christ, you have reconciled yourself to all of creation. By your Spirit, you are with us, working to reconcile us all to you. Because you are holy, you long to bring your kingdom near, to fulfil your purpose within the new creation, to render in fullness your word of peace. This is your purpose, your divine mercy, and you will accomplish it.

We need to know and live into the fullness of your peace. We have lived as if you were our enemy. We have assumed that our power and authority is your power and authority. We have let sin, brokenness and the lies of the prince of this world define the path for our feet. We confess that we continue to choose darkness instead of light, to hide in fear of you, rather than believe and trust in your desire to draw us near.

O Holy One, open our hearts to the truth, that we might see you in the light of Jesus, who loved you with his whole being. By your Spirit, may we see the world through the eyes of our reconciling Christ, who entrusts us with his ministry of reconciliation for your sake. You who have overcome, this is your desire, your work, your glory.

We make our peace with you, that we might become messengers of your peace. Heal us and heal this world through us. Use our hands to build your new creation. May your kingdom come on earth, as it is in heaven. Amen.

1

Dimensions of the healing ministry

In this chapter we seek to do a number of things. First of all, we remember the many healing themes embedded in the biblical story, where we take note of the comprehensive nature of healing. Healing is not simply the removal of pain or the solving of a problem, but rather an entry into greater wholeness of life through God's grace and goodness.

Second, we trace the healing themes and ministries exercised by the Christian Church over its long journey in history. The diversity and richness of these themes highlight that there is not one single path to healing, but rather many forms of healing and numerous ways in which greater wholeness may come to us. For example, when we are healed from our inner wounding, that healing will flow into our relationships with others. For when we are more at peace within ourselves, we will be less reactive when we relate to others.

Third, we introduce our vision and strategies for praying inner-healing prayers. By focusing on inner healing, we do not mean to imply that this is the *most* important form of healing. Rather, the Church seems to be less familiar with this form of healing prayers. Most church formularies, such as the *Catechism of the Catholic Church*[1] and *An Australian Prayer Book*,[2] speak of the importance of the healing ministry of the Church, yet they give scant attention to inner-healing prayers.

Healing themes in the biblical story

In order to understand the specific themes of healing throughout the biblical narrative, we first must recognize the central narrative scheme of the Bible: Creation, chaos or the Fall and re-creation.

1

Creation speaks of God's participation in all that exists and heralds the goodness of our world. The theme of chaos, or the Fall, speaks about humanity's disobedience, sinfulness and woundedness in all its personal and social dimensions. This means not only that I sin against others and that others sin against me, but also that I live in social conditions that may harm me. The dark side of a culture or the psychopathology of an institution may affect me in ways that call for healing. Thus our need for healing comes not only from personal relationships going astray and the negative work of satanic forces, but also from the brokenness of our world. Consequently, chaos, or the Fall, constitutes the precondition of our need for healing and restoration. The work of re-creation, redemption and restoration is the movement of healing that leads us from brokenness into wholeness through God's provision for us in Christ. Therefore, healing is not a sub-theme in the biblical story, but rather the key to the new creation that lies at the heart of the mystery of the in-breaking reign of God. Thus healing is not only personal, but also institutional and societal as well as eschatological, for it anticipates the healing of all things. Moreover, healing is not restricted to certain parts of the biblical narrative, but is woven throughout the whole mosaic of Scripture.

The Old Testament biblical mosaic of healing

One does not need to travel very far into the Bible before one meets the astounding declaration, 'I am the LORD who heals you' (Exodus 15.26). The setting for this description of the nature of Yahweh has to do with the provision of sweet water to sustain life (v. 25), the call to obey God's ways (v. 26) and the promise of a life of freedom and blessing without the diseases brought on Egypt (v. 26). Clearly, God's vision for healing is much wider than overcoming a personal physical ailment. The healing vision here is communal, life-sustaining, preventative and suggests a general sense of well-being – perhaps best summed up in the word *shalom*, which recurs throughout the Old Testament.

The theme of healing is also important in the prophetic writings. Perhaps the fullest articulation occurs in Isaiah 61.1–4, where personal and communal healing ('bind up the broken-hearted' and 'comfort all who mourn', giving them 'the mantle of praise instead of a faint spirit') is complemented by social freedom ('proclaim liberty to captives'), which results in social transformation ('they shall build up the ancient ruins'). In this vision of healing, the promise of wholeness is both personal and communal, impacting one's internal life as well as one's social conditions.

While there are instances in the Old Testament of the healing of individuals (2 Kings 20.5; Jeremiah 17.14; Psalm 6.2), the broader vision is for personal and communal restoration (Hosea 6.1; Jeremiah 33.6; Isaiah 6.10; Ezekiel 34.16). The Old Testament has in view a healing of all relationships and a life of communal solidarity and care. This vision of healing brings with it particular challenges for those living in the self-preoccupied and individualistic Western world – including the Church – where healing is primarily thought of as personal relief from sickness. Yet the Wisdom literature of the biblical narrative traces a rich tapestry of the healing actions of Yahweh, identifying physical healing (Psalms 6.2; 41.3), spiritual healing (Psalm 41.4), general well-being and encouragement (Proverbs 12.1; 16.24), inner healing (Psalm 147.3), and communal deliverance and restoration (Psalm 107.19–20).

Key New Testament themes

The New Testament is equally comprehensive in its understanding of the healing ministry of Christ, which the early Christian communities carried forward into the world through the power of the Spirit. Though the New Testament builds on the Old Testament, much of the contemporary writing about the healing ministry neglects the Old Testament and uses the New Testament as the starting point for understanding Christian healing.[3]

Luke returns to Isaiah's vision of healing (61.1–4) in his Gospel (4.17–19). This healing manifesto becomes the framework for the entire Gospel and differentiates the ministry of Jesus from that of John the Baptist (Luke 7.22–23). Luke recounts many narratives about the healing of individuals (Luke 4.38–39; 5.12–13; 6.6–11; 7.1–10), and he clearly defines the mission of Jesus and his disciples as one of proclamation and healing (Luke 6.17–19; 9.1–2). Luke clarifies the healing ministry in a number of ways. He distinguishes between healing an illness and the ministry of deliverance, where evil spirits are identified and commanded to leave (Luke 9.1). Furthermore, he draws a connection between the forgiveness of sins and physical healing (Luke 5.17–26). He also points out that these healings reflect the in-breaking reign of God (Luke 9.11). In other words, healings are not an end in themselves, concerned simply with curing people, but are a pathway into the kingdom of God (Luke 10.9), where his followers embrace God's grace and reign and step into a new way of living. This in-breaking of God's reign challenges those who think they have no need (Luke 18.24). It also calls for costly renunciation (Luke 18.29–30) and invites us into the practice of radical hospitality (Luke 14.15–24).

Luke continues these themes in his Acts of the Apostles, where he makes it clear that the early Church is called to continue the ministry inaugurated by Jesus. Like Jesus, the early Christians carry out this ministry in the power of the Spirit (Luke 3.21–22; 4.1; 11.20; Acts 10.38; 1.8; 3.16). Thus in the praxis of the early Christian communities, we hear accounts of both physical healing and exorcisms (Acts 3.6–7; 5.16; 9.33–34; 14.8–10; 28.8–9).

Other New Testament passages illuminate additional aspects of healing by the power of the Spirit, which are reflected in the particular charisms that the Spirit gives to members of the community of faith (1 Corinthians 12.9, 28, 30). Healing is also identified as a sacramental ministry that involves the laying on of hands (Luke 4.40), anointing with oil (James 4.14), prayers of faith (James 4.15), confession of sin (James 4.16) and the involvement of church elders (James 5.14).

As we discuss specific examples of healing prayers in later chapters, these biblical themes will guide us, for as contemporary practitioners of the healing ministry, we must root ourselves in the witness of biblical testimony.

Healing strategies in the Church

We must now make a long leap from the ancient stories of the healing ministry of Jesus and the early Church to our contemporary situation. Morton Kelsey has traced this history and concludes,

'There is a great gulf between the modern Christian attitude toward healing and that of the early church.'[4] While we will not pursue this history here, we do agree with Kelsey's vision for contemporary manifestations of Christian healing when he notes, 'It [healing] will come through the Eucharistic fellowship . . . through . . . individuals endowed with special gifts of healing. It will come through teaching and preaching, as well as from the direct activity of the Spirit through prayer.'[5] What this means is that healing can come in a variety of ways, and so it is appropriate to speak of various forms or dimensions of healing, which we will briefly summarize in the following pages.

Spiritual healing

The biblical framework for healing makes it clear that the most important dimension of healing is not physical – although this aspect is certainly important – but rather the spiritual restoration of our relationship with God. This work of grace in Christ through the Spirit overcomes our alienation and brings us into a dynamic relationship with the Trinity.

Thus salvation is healing, and the initial movement of this healing is homecoming, which is expressed beautifully in Paul's vision of being welcomed into God's covenant of grace (Ephesians 2.11–14). The ongoing movement of this restorative healing continues as we grow into Christian maturity and the graces and virtues of the Christian life (Galatians 5.22–23) and also in conformity to Christ and his way of being in the world (Ephesians 4.13). When our greatest hurt is healed, we experience God's salvation in Christ. Thus the word of grace has healing power. This is expressed in the lectionary reading on Luke. 'Almighty God, who inspired Luke the physician to proclaim the love and healing power of your Son: give your Church, by the grace of the Spirit and through the medicine of the gospel, the same love and power to heal.'[6] The gospel is medicine, indeed.

Relational healing

Spiritual healing is a movement of transcendence that shapes our vertical relationship with God. Relational healing moves horizontally into the world and transforms our relationships. Thus our relationship with God shapes and determines our relationships with others as we seek to embody forgiveness in our lives, as we embrace the joy of friendship, or as we pick up the tasks of peacemaking and building community.

Relational healing connects the healing of our relationship with God to our own inner healing so that our responses to others do not come from places of alienation and wounding, but rather from the good spaces of God's healing kindness. Having come home to God as the Trinity, we can come home to others. Having been invited into the life of God as a community, we can build the human community and the community of faith.

This form of ongoing healing invites us into the heart of the Lord's Prayer: 'forgive us our debts, as we also have forgiven our debtors' (Matthew 6.12). It also invites us into radical reconciliation (Luke 6.27–31). Moreover, relational healing reminds us that our link to God binds us in love and responsibility to others (1 Corinthians 12.12–13), and this is to be outworked in a radical redefining of our relationships: 'Jews or Greeks, slaves or free . . . we were all made to drink of one Spirit' (1 Corinthians 12.13). In other words, the old social differences and tribalisms have to go. In Christ, we must establish new relationships (Galatians 4.27–28), which make possible the new humanity, where Christ as the second Adam shows us a new way (1 Corinthians 15.22). Healing, therefore, is critical in friendship and community building. So often, we go about hurting others because we ourselves have never dealt with our own hurts. When our hurts are healed, we become candidates for relationship and friendship.

Physical healing

Physical healing reminds us of God's total concern for humanity and that our spirituality is not only for the inner person, but the whole person. As such, physical healing expresses God's materiality towards us and is a small sign of the movement of the Incarnation and the resurrection.

As we have seen, various forms of healing, including physical healing, are very much a part of the biblical witness. Traditionally, the Church has linked physical healing with prayer (Psalms 103.1–3; 30.2; James 5.14), the confession of sins (Psalms 41.4; 51.8–9; James 5.16), the laying on of hands (Luke 4.40), and anointing with oil (Mark 6.13; James 5.14). Physical healing has been part of the long history of the Church's ministry, although this has fluctuated over time. For example, during the Council of Trent in 1551, the healing ministry in the Church was weakened when extreme unction was established as a service in preparation for death, rather than as a service for healing, which had been the earlier practice.[7] With the Second Vatican Council (1962–5), the Sacrament of the Anointing of the Sick was restored to the life of the Church.

Certainly, physical healing is a complex phenomenon. The body has its own healing and restorative properties, and exercise and other preventive interventions (including mental and spiritual practices) can aid in our physical well-being. In the modern world, the focus for physical restoration has shifted to medical interventions, for which we are deeply grateful. This has impacted the healing ministry of the Church, where there is no longer a strong emphasis on healing the sick, apart from among a few Pentecostal groups. Yet 'Part of the plan laid out by God's providence is that we should fight strenuously against all sickness and carefully seek the blessings of good health so that we may fulfil our role in human society and the church.'[8]

Inner healing

The premise of the inner-healing ministry is that we are often emotionally wounded as we journey through life. Others may intentionally hurt us, or they may unintentionally hurt us through the unfortunate things they say and do. Even decades later, we can continue to be affected deeply by what others have said or done to us. As a consequence, we often react and respond to others in ways that mirror how we ourselves have been hurt. Over time, our inner wounds and outward responses can become part of who we are and how we act in the world.

If we never process these inner wounds, we will not be able to live out of the grace and freedom of Christ. Prayers for inner healing recognize that through the presence of the Holy Spirit,

Jesus Christ wants to bring his healing presence into those wounded places. The ministry of an inner-healing prayer team can help those who are in difficult places and who need to face their wounds and open them before God so that they can live proactively, rather than reactively, into the future.

This form of healing is rooted in the biblical story. Though the term inner healing is not used, it is a large part of the biblical witness. Psalms 69.20; 38.5; Jeremiah 8.11, 22; 14.17; 30.12–13, among other passages of Scripture, speak of various forms of personal and national wounding. Psalm 103.3 makes the link between confession of sin and physical healing. Psalm 34.18 speaks of Yahweh's love and care for the broken-hearted. The line from Psalm 147.3, 'He heals the broken-hearted, and binds up their wounds', occurs in the setting of national restoration (see 147.2). Clearly, for the biblical authors, there is a connection between personal healing and corporate healing, because coming to an inner peace was part of their understanding of what Yahweh sought to do for his people.

The language of healing in the New Testament is quite different. There is a clear connection between forgiveness of sins and healing (Mark 2.10–11; James 5.16), along with a clear distinction between physical healing and the ministry of deliverance from oppressive forces (Luke 9.1–2). But when we come to the matter of inner healing, the New Testament uses the more general language of restoration, healing, wholeness and freedom. Key passages include Luke 4.18–19, Romans 6.17–18, 2 Corinthians 5.17, Galatians 5.16, Ephesians 4.25–27, 5.8. But in the book of Colossians, we are told that we have to embrace, put on, appropriate and live into the new life that we have received through Christ (Colossians 3.1–17). Living into this new life involves dealing with our sins and woundedness so that Christ may more fully live in us.

The ministry of inner healing is also reflected in the early traditions of the Church, such as in the preparation for Christian initiation through the catechesis, confession of faith, baptism, prayer for the infilling of the Holy Spirit, anointing with oil for healing, and prayers of exorcism.[9] And inner healing is also part of the longer tradition of soul care and spiritual direction.[10] More recently, inner healing has come to the forefront through the pioneering ministry of Agnes Sanford, an Episcopalian lay woman, who reminds the Church in the modern world that Christ not only healed in his earthly ministry, but continues to heal today through the Spirit.[11] This healing is not only for the soul, but also for the body and for inner brokenness.

The ministry of inner healing recognizes that we are not made up of disparate parts – body, soul and spirit – and therefore we cannot minister to one dimension of a person without accounting for other aspects of humanity. The healing ministry embraces the whole human person, what John Polkinghorne refers to as a 'psychosomatic unity, an animated body'.[12] Thus sin and wounding not only affect us spiritually, but also emotionally, physically and relationally.

Healing of the demonized

This dimension of healing continues to create many problems for modern Christians. As Zygmunt Bauman notes, this resistance stems in part from the modern commitment to a rational, objectivist and scientistic world-view, with its arrogance that 'everything receding into the past is ... backward, retrograde, inferior'.[13] Thus the ancient world-view, which includes 'the world' of the biblical narrative and its view of miracles and the demonic, is outmoded and irrelevant.

This modern world-view has also impacted the Church. As Morton Kelsey points out, 'there is a great gulf between the modern Christian attitude toward healing and that of the early church ... Indeed, the difference is so pronounced that one wonders how two such divergent views could have developed within the same institution.'[14] Some Protestant scholarship has clearly not helped, such as Rudolf Bultmann's assertion that '*The idea of a miracle* has, therefore, become untenable and *it must be abandoned*',[15] a perspective that embraces the modern world-view above one of the key dynamics of the gospel story. While we need to recognize that the writers of the biblical story were historically situated, this is also true of us. Thus we should not readily dismiss past authors simply because we moderns are somehow more enlightened. We need to be particularly careful that we don't psychologize biblical texts by making demonic oppression a psychological illness. On the other hand, we need to be equally careful that we don't make every personal problem a demonic oppression.

The Gospel of Luke makes it clear that Jesus ministered to people who were oppressed by demonic entities (Luke 8.2; 8.35; 11.20; 13.16; 13.32), and the 'Nazareth Manifesto' speaks of 'release to the captives' (Luke 4.18). The gospel narrative also makes it clear that Jesus entrusted this ministry of deliverance to his followers (Luke 9.1; 10.17–20).

Paul further explains the role of the demonic in human affairs, noting that sin has a threefold source. We sin because we are caught up in the fallen ways of the world, because we give in to our own sinful nature, and because we are influenced by demonic forces (Ephesians 2.1–3). In referring to the latter, Paul speaks of 'following the ruler of the power of the air' (Ephesians 2.2). He continues by saying that Christians should not give the evil one room and opportunity to gain a foothold in their lives (Ephesians 4.27), and he explains how demonic forces need to be resisted (Ephesians 6.10–17).

In the early church tradition, exorcism was an important part of Christian initiation, as described in the Apostolic Tradition of Hippolytus. The candidate for baptism was asked to say, 'I renounce you, Satan, and all your service and all your works.' After this confession, the presbyter would anoint the candidate with the oil of exorcism, saying, 'May every spirit depart from you.'[16] This baptismal practice is still used today in mainline liturgical churches, including the Roman Catholic Church.[17] For persons manifesting some form of demonic activity in their lives, the Catholic Church performs special exorcisms under strict guidelines.[18]

In more contemporary practice, prayers for deliverance are said for persons within the framework of confession and healing prayers. Such prayers may be necessary for those who have become oppressed in some way, those who have opened themselves to occult practices, or those who have had curses called upon them in the name of Satan or the devil.[19]

Healing of society

The vision of societal healing flows from the above forms of healing, as those who experience healing become more able to extend grace, forgiveness and goodness to others.[20] As Paul writes, the God who comforts us also empowers us to comfort others (2 Corinthians 1.4).

Yet this is not a crusade, and the vision to bring healing to our world cannot be cast in triumphalistic terms, for we are not Messiahs, but rather mere witnesses to what God can do. And yet in wisdom, God has chosen to work with us and through us. So we are called to build community in our neighbourhoods and to befriend our neighbours. We are also called to be a healing presence within our work situations and wherever we find ourselves. This means that we live as peacemakers, persons of grace and forgiveness, workers for reconciliation, carers for those who are struggling and facing difficulties. Because of the great love God has shown us in Christ, we are called to extend that same goodness and love to others – both those outside the faith community as well as those who are our sisters and brothers in Christ (Galatians 6.10; Luke 6.32–36).

We are talking here about the mission of the whole people of God to bring the whole gospel in word and deed to the whole world.[21] Or, to put that in different terms, we are the bearers of the kingdom of God, and as such we are called to be the sign, servant and sacrament of the reign of God to others. As a sign, we point others to the grace of God. As servants, we commit ourselves to do the will of God in serving his kingdom purposes. And as a sacrament, we may say to others, come and see something of the goodness of God among us. The Franciscan lectionary puts this rather well when citing Psalm 67 and inviting us to pray: 'Let your ways be known upon the earth, your saving health among all the nations' (v. 2). Then it cites the liberating vision of Isaiah: 'I have given you as a covenant to the people, a light to the nations, to open the eyes that are blind, to bring out the captives from the dungeon, from prison, those who sit in darkness' (Isaiah 42.5–6). Then it cites a canticle, 'This is the Christ, the Chosen of God, the one who will bring healing to the nations.'[22]

11

This calling to be a healing presence in our deeply conflicted and wounded world is embedded in the biblical narrative. The prophet Jeremiah, while speaking about national restoration out of captivity, declares the healing word of the Lord: 'I am going to bring it recovery and healing; I will heal them and reveal to them abundance of prosperity and security' (Jeremiah 33.6). This reflects part of the comprehensive meaning of the term *shalom* in the Old Testament. And this wider vision of healing is broached by Peter when he writes, 'He himself bore our sins in his body on the cross, so that, free from sins, we might live for righteousness; by his wounds you have been healed' (1 Peter 2.24). Having been healed in the grace of Christ, we are invited to live righteous lives, lives of goodness and care for others.

The missional calling of the people of God and the invitation to be the servants of Christ cannot emerge from our activism alone, but must first come out of grace, healing and contemplation.[23] Because contemplative practices are not only revelatory but also reflective, these practices open up the dark spaces in our lives, just as much as they give us energy and focus for a life of witness and service. Agnes Sanford, the 'godmother' of modern healing prayers, recognizes that healing prayers are not simply for our own interiority, but have a wider significance of blessing and renewal for society. In her own idiosyncratic way, she writes, 'So we have gone deep in repentance for our own sins that we may be better channels for the forgiveness of national sins.'[24]

This calls to mind the great national prayer of Solomon: 'If my people who are called by my name humble themselves, pray, seek my face, and turn from their wicked ways, then I will hear from heaven, and will forgive their sin and heal their land' (2 Chronicles 7.14). It also echoes the confessional and restorative prayer of Nehemiah: 'let your ear be attentive and your eyes open to hear the prayer of your servant that I now pray before you day and night for your servants, the people of Israel, confessing the sins of the people of Israel which we have sinned against you' (Nehemiah 1.6). While the healing of society can come through many instrumentalities, including the political and the economic, the processes of relational healing and community building play a significant part in bringing about a societal shalom.

Healing of the land

One of the more controversial dimensions of healing prayers is whether or not we should pray for the creation. Or, in other words, whether ecological healing should be part of our personal and corporate prayer life. Agnes Sanford writes, 'I believe with all my heart that prayer *can* affect the creation,' and so she prayed for decades for the healing of the San Andreas fault line along the Californian coast.[25] Praying for the land also occurs among Christians who live in vulnerable natural areas, such as near volcanoes or in the regular path of cyclones or tornadoes. Filipino Christians living in the Visayas pray for the minimization of destructive typhoons that yearly devastate all of their crops and bring widespread flooding in their wake.

There is no reason why such praying should not occur. In fact, in the Western Church, we need to relearn the language and art of prayer as the breath of the life of the Christian. Richard Foster speaks of prayer as finding the heart's true home.[26] And prayer cannot and should not concern a narrow set of issues, such as my needs, or spiritual matters alone. Prayer should be about all of life – certainly our lives, but also our homes and backyards, our places of work and spaces of recreation, our neighbourhoods and our nations, along with the farming community, our forests and the land.

In recovering our prayer life for the land, Celtic spirituality is particularly informative and suggestive. There are prayers for the land and for farming, for the sea and the stars. One prayer makes the connection with nature clear: 'Who is there on land? Who is there on wave? Who is there on billow? Who is there by door-post? Who is along with us? God and Lord.'[27]

There are, of course, many practical ways in which our prayers for the healing of the land must translate into responsible and sustainable stewardship of the earth and its resources, assuming personal responsibility for the ways in which we use power and water in our homes and the ways in which we use our gardens and other urban spaces. As we think and pray and work in this way, we begin to see the sacred interconnectedness of all of life. Homes, transport systems, the rural community and its farming practices, recreational spaces, industry – a list that is long and wide – all speak to us about the call for a careful sustainability of God's earth and its resources, made all the more urgent in the light of global climate change and population growth.

Even though Agnes Sanford is rightly regarded as a Christian mystic, and her prayers for the healing of the land may seem somewhat strange, she was nevertheless practical as well. She writes:

> If we have cut down forests that nature needs in order to draw rain, then there is no use in beating on the doors of heaven unless we do all we can to awaken those in authority to the need of reforestation.[28]

Thus she recognizes that advocacy is an important part of healing prayers.

Healing of the dying

Though this form of healing prayer may seem somewhat contradictory, it demonstrates that healing strategies need to inform all the dimensions of life – and this includes death. We all know from personal experience that crises within family systems due to the death of a family member can throw up major unresolved problems, leading to conflict precisely at a time when the family should pull together. Thus the impending death of a family member opens up an opportunity for care and reconciliation.

This form of healing prayer helps prepare a dying person for a good death by nurturing thoughtful medical care and pain management as well as caring and reconciled relationships with family and friends. The long history of the hospice movement reflects something of this vision.[29] Because so much of life has become technologized, particularly the medical profession, there is a growing need for relational reconciliation and healing among those who are dying and those who are left behind. Here again, we are calling for a recovery of the earlier vision of the community of faith being a place of grace, care and healing.

Eschatological healing

As a metanarrative, the biblical story moves from the theme of creation to that of chaos and fall to the final theme of the new creation: a grand vision of the restoration of all things in the new heavens and a new earth. The theme of the healing of persons and nations and the whole created order is held within that eschatological vision. Thus the theme of healing is never a minor note in the biblical story, but rather the final crescendo.

The grand healing theme is prefigured in Isaiah's vision of restoration (Isaiah 11.1–9; 65.17–25) and later in the Pauline vision of a Christocentric healing of all things: 'to reconcile to himself all things, whether on earth or in heaven, by making peace through the blood of his cross' (Colossians 1.20). But the final unfolding of this grand theme appears in Revelation, where there is no more pain and death (Revelation 21.4), and where there is the complete healing of the nations (Revelation 22.2). This suggests that the themes of restoration, renewal and healing are intrinsic to the biblical story and form its essential narrative.

Yet we have grossly neglected restoration, renewal and healing in the modern Church, particularly in the wider sense envisioned in the biblical narrative. To that extent, we have failed to live well and more fully into the biblical story, and we have possibly blunted the relevance of the ministry of the Church – not only towards its own, but also in its mission to the world.

Conclusion

In this chapter we have sought to trace the biblical vision of healing in Scripture, noting its comprehensive nature both in the Old Testament and the New Testament and also how the whole created order is to bear the healing marks of God, moving from the personal to the communal. We have also described the diverse forms of healing within the faith community and have identified how these dimensions are connected and inter-related. Thus we understand how the healing ministry is not simply for one's migraine headache, but rather for the inner, outer and relational healing of the whole person – body, mind and spirit.

In writing this book, we are calling for a recovery of this biblical vision and for a recovery of a fuller practice of the healing ministry in the contemporary Church. To this end, we seek to empower our readers into the spaces of prayer that will connect us more fully with the restorative passion that lies in the heart of God and should be our hope and dream.

ༀ

Jesus,

you inaugurated the new kingdom with your earth-walking days, breaking this world's bondage and decay with your life-giving act of forgiveness. Your love broke the power of sin. Your death and resurrection marked the way of the new creation. As John said, you are the light of the world.

We are your people, the body of Christ, made to receive your love and to be transformed through your love, that we might become a light to the nations and bring peace to the world.

But we have lost the way. We are like scattered sheep and cannot find your path of peace. In our fear, we have run from your healing and hidden our wounds from you. In our bitterness, we have refused the hope of your reconciliation. In our pride, we have controlled the gospel in order to build our own version of peace. In our confusion, we have sought to restore and redeem the world for our glory, not yours.

Lord have mercy. Christ have mercy. Lord have mercy.

We are alone, and our lives are filled with strife. We have set ourselves against each other and against you. We no longer live by the grace of your salvation, and so we cannot proclaim your good news.

Lord, have mercy. Christ, have mercy. Lord, have mercy.

Light of the world, reveal the disease within us that separates us from you.

Illuminate your path of peace, that we might return to you and be cleansed and healed by your living presence within us and through us. Restore the good news of forgiveness and comfort, reconciliation and restoration to your Church. Through us, may you build up the ancient ruins and raise up the former devastations; may you repair the ruined cities and the devastations of many generations.

God of all mercy and compassion, humble us with your abundant love, that we might go forth into the darkness of the world, bearing the bright beacon of your light and the fullness of your healing.

By the power of your Holy Spirit, may your kingdom come, may your peace abound, for the glory of your holy name. Amen.

2

A case study

———◆•◆———

This is the story of James (not his real name, but his story, nonetheless). It is not the full story of his healing, as that would involve the whole of James's life's journey, even into God's eschatological future. The story focuses on a transitional time in James's life when he was able, over time, to open up about his inner wounding. Thus this case study is primarily about inner-healing prayers, though his story clearly involves other forms of healing.

When James was in his early thirties, he came to live as a volunteer in one of our youth facilities working with juvenile delinquents. Our organization worked in urban mission with homeless youth and people in the drug scene.[1] A thoughtful, capable, helpful young man, James soon proved to be an asset to the facility and settled in well with the staff and volunteers as well as the challenging youth with whom we worked.

After many months, James began to develop a relationship with one of the female staff members and later came for general pastoral counselling. During those initial discussions, his presenting issues were his shyness and his uncertainty about how to carry the relationship forward.

Some time later, James came for further advice and counsel. During these conversations, he brought up his troubled background, including his difficulties in secondary school and his suicidal tendencies. These revelations indicated that James was involved in reflective work and seeking to process his past, as he had concluded that his past had something to do with the challenges in his present relationships. He observed that whenever he came close to someone, he immediately began to withdraw.

So far, this story invites careful reflection. From the above, we can see that James did not come to counselling requesting healing prayers, but rather he expressed concern about certain dimensions of his present relationships and how his past continued to influence him in the present. This scenario is typical, in that most church-goers do not know of their need for healing prayers – and may not ever have heard about such prayers. But generally, those who are involved in the life of the Church and recognize their need for counselling are very open to receiving healing prayers, whenever this seems necessary and relevant. This is not to suggest that every-one seeking help needs healing prayers, for there are many ways that people can be helped – formally and informally, spiritually and psychologically. Therefore, we must exercise careful discern-ment when we invite a person for healing prayers.

Over time, James sought further help and counsel for these and other issues. As he began to be in touch with several difficult child-hood experiences, his journey began to take some significant turns. By exploring together a number of related memories that high-lighted the problem of emotional abuse, we came to the conclusion that healing prayers would be appropriate. When James was ready to proceed, this emotional abuse became the focus for healing prayers. In the following, we trace the central arc of James's story.

৪০০৪

James lived with his parents in a farmhouse in a rural area, where they were sugar cane farmers. One Friday afternoon, the whole rural community came together for the annual school sports day. In silence, James's parents drove him the hour to the school. With no sense of joyful anticipation regarding the day's outing, James felt uncomfortable and tense. James ruefully identified his family by this difficult silence that hung every day over the family home-stead. His father tended his work, brooding in sullen silence and suppressed anger. His mother seldom said anything personal, although she was a good mother practically.

James was not a sports hero, but a bookworm who loved read-ing and enjoyed being by himself. His participation in the sports events of that day did not go well – either in the team events or in his sprints in the 100 and 200 metres. During the day's events, he did not see his parents until it was time to return to the farm. They rode home in an even more brooding and electric silence, with no one speaking a word. James felt relief when the homestead came into view. He would feed the chickens, collect the eggs, and possibly have time to go to the dam and watch the ducks in their peaceful play before it was time for dinner. The dam was a sacred place for him, not the home.

After parking the car in the shed, everyone got out. Then James's father grabbed him roughly by the scruff of the neck and yelled, 'I'll teach you to be a good son of mine and a real man.' He dragged James to the holding paddock in front of the homestead and said, 'Run until you drop.'

In the late afternoon, with the sun already dipping towards the skyline, James began running up and down the paddock, feeling bewildered, angry and confused. He knew his father was unhappy that he had come near to last in his races, but he always seemed to be unhappy with everything that James did. He had never commended James for anything, let alone for doing well academically.

Dusk fell suddenly, as it does in the subtropics, and the hills in the distance began to fade. As James stumbled around the paddock in the pitch dark, the night silence crept over the summer landscape. After he finally collapsed, James crawled into the house and then into his bed. During that long night, no one came to see him, hold him or comfort him – not even his mother.

The next morning, they ate breakfast as usual. No one spoke. No one asked questions or explained anything. The dreaded silence filled the house, which echoed with unresolved issues and tension. Yet for James, life did not go on as before. As a 13-year-old, James did not understand nor have words for what was happening to him, yet he was deeply wounded by his father's rejection and abuse.

This became a primal wounding for James, and during the new year at secondary school, James became distracted and his academic work suffered. A loner, James became depressed and eventually, towards the end of secondary school, suicidal. But life went on, and there was no intervention, counselling or healing, which brings us to when we met James and he was finally able to tell his story.

Again, the story calls for further reflection. Inner wounding is part of life for most people. At some point, we will be hurt by what others say and do to us – whether in our family setting, school, work or neighbourhood. And, of course, we will all end up hurting others. Some hurts are like water off a duck's back, and we shrug them off. This is just as well, otherwise we would be overwhelmingly burdened. But other wounds deeply scar us, as when James experienced his father's rejection and abuse on that 'fatal' day.

ಹಃಇಃ

For most of us, life goes on, and we try to forget or suppress our hurts, rather than process them along the way. Yet the hurts remain, underground fissures running beneath the surface of our lives. If we are not attentive to the ways these wounds mark us, they will erupt into our present stories, often in unrecognizable ways. But for James some recognition had come. When James was ready to own and share his story, he opened a pathway for the brooding Spirit to begin the work of recovery and restoration. This is what the rest of this book is all about.

None of us comes easily to the place where we own and face our inner wounding. Often, present difficulties open the way for us to reflect on what we may have pushed aside or buried. But whatever the reasons or circumstances, when we come to this place of insight and openness, we enter the arena of grace. Though it may take years for us to come to this place, when we do, we are on the doorstep of a renewed life. Following are several prayers for those who are seeking to come to the light.

ಹಃಇಃ

O God,

I hear you calling, and it both frightens and draws me. I want to run from you, and yet I want you to shelter me.

Will you reject me? Will you announce my secret that I am not who I want everyone to think I am? Will you reveal that I am not who others expect me to be? Will you expose my judgement of others? Will you judge me?

I cannot bear your condemnation. So I will hide from you, because I am afraid of you.

And yet I hear you calling me, and there is no hate in your voice, only tenderness. I hear you saying that there is no condemnation for those who believe, and I long to step towards your light. You have been calling me for such a long time.

Do you see something in me that I cannot see? Do you have hope in me that will release me from my fears and judgements and from all that keeps me from life? Will you comfort me and keep me safe? Hope is rising in me. I long to know more of your love.

O God, keep calling. I choose to trust you. Bring your light into my life. Come as you promise and search my deepest, hidden places. Only grant me the honesty that rests in your mercy and answers my fears with Love itself. Amen.

᪥

Spirit of the Living God,

you go where you will, always tuned to the depths of pain, to the darkest edge of forsakenness. You are not afraid, for your living love will let nothing separate us from you. You have known these deep places, these darkest nights, since the beginning of time, and you contain them, holding all within your brooding self, groaning for their completion into life by the hand of God.

Come, Holy Spirit. Come. Come into each place that needs your mending, life-building, breath-giving ways. We watch for you. We wait for you, for you are our hope of the morning. Amen.

᪥

Spirit of God,

from the beginning of time, when you swept over the face of
the waters, you have been calling forth the word of God into
our world and lighting the darkness. You, who groan with the
holy weight of God's love and longing, come. We hope in your
seeking. We listen for your call. We wait for you. Come, Spirit of
God. Come and move into our stories. Come into the darkness
that we both fear and hide within. Come into the burdens that
crush us. Come into our lies and sin and reveal the truth to us.
Come and free us. Comforter who heals, we open our hearts
and hands to receive you. Amen.

ଈଓଔଷ

Jesus,

I don't want to remember the things I've been trying so hard
to forget. I don't want to think about the experiences I've been
trying to live down.

Yet I am so tired of living with this aching regret and piercing
condemnation. I am so weary of being angry and hating. I am
so sick of lies. I hate the fear that keeps pushing me around. I
am so sad about the ways I have used my hurt to hurt others.
I want my life to be different.

If your Spirit can meet me where I only feel pain, come. If you
can heal me where I feel broken, come. If you can show me
a way where I can see no way, come. If you can resurrect
life where I only know death, come. If you can redeem the
experiences I want to forget, come, Lord Jesus, come. Here is
my hand. I take your hand. Guard me and help me. Soften my
heart and show me the way to your promise of life. Amen.

3

Preparation prayers

—•·•·•—

As we move further into James's healing story, we want to emphasize how important the preparation time is for the ministry of
inner healing. Since this ministry is like open-heart surgery, the
prayer team should not just jump into a prayer session, and the
person coming for prayer should not be totally surprised by what
happens during those sessions. Both the counsellee and the prayer
team must be adequately prepared for the prayer ministry time
by sharing key information with one another beforehand and by
making space to pray both for the person who will come for help
and also for those who will minister.

Introduction

In this chapter, we will connect the preparation time with James's
story. Then we will offer general guidelines about how to prepare
someone for healing prayers. These guidelines can be applied
to a range of situations. Finally, we will explore how to discern
whether or not a person should proceed with healing prayers and
how to process the timing for those prayer sessions. Throughout,
we will share some sample prayers that can guide you as you
nurture this ministry in your particular context.

To begin, we must emphasize that healing prayers are not to be
cast in crisis terms, though we might be stirred to pray healing
prayers spontaneously in many such situations. We might quietly
pray for healing for a particular student in class or a colleague at
work, or we might pray for a fellow church member at the close
of a service or with a friend over a cup of coffee.

Yet in these settings, there are obvious limitations of time and
place. One could hardly pray adequately for James over a cup of

coffee. Without adequate preparation, such spontaneous prayers can become preparatory in and of themselves. For example, after a worship service, if someone shares their experience of a wounding in a present relationship, we should certainly offer prayer for that person and situation. But then we must offer pastoral follow-up and set aside further time for healing prayer.

Following are two possible prayers for a spontaneous ministry time in any situation. By way of example, we have used James's name in these prayers.

ℰℭ

Lord,

you have promised that you are present whenever two or three are gathered in your name. Here we are. Thank you for being with us.

I lift up James's tender story to you and ask you to encompass it with your love and attend to it with your grace. As your Spirit moves into the darkness of his hurt, restore it with your cleansing light. Work your way into the depths of this story and bring James comfort and peace.

Protect James from the liar of this world, who would try to convince him that nothing can bring healing to his story. We place your light around James like a cloak and ask your Spirit to guard him and keep him safe from all harm.

We trust you, and we place James's life and story into your goodness and your safekeeping, as you continue to brood within him and around him, redeeming, healing and reconciling all you have made with your love. Amen.

ℰℭ

Dear Jesus,

thank you that there are no depths that you have not descended, and there is no sin or difficulty whose weight you have not borne. For at the cross, you held all pain, fear and confusion, and nothing falls outside your power of life and grace. In this moment, relieve James from the fear that you will not, or cannot, take his story on. Remind him that nothing can separate him from your powerful love. By your Spirit, comfort him and tenderly speak your word of truth to him.

Thank you for receiving all our prayers and confessions into your spacious mercy. Sort through the pain and fear that surrounds James's story. Soften his heart and give him the strength to follow your leading along the path of peace you have stretched out before him.

Thank you for your gentleness and humility. We trust that your burden for James will be light. May your love and healing presence give James courage and hope. May your mercy and grace be the food and drink that sustains him. Amen.

ଽଠେଓ

Preparing James for inner healing

As we have noted, James was led over a long period of time to seek healing prayers. Typically, people don't tap you on the shoulder asking for healing prayers – not even in the life of the community of faith. More often, as the Spirit works in the lives of those who are on a personal journey of recovery and renewal, nurturing their faith and courage, they begin to identify and face things in their lives that are affecting them in the present.

We should not think of healing prayers as archaeological expeditions that draw people into unhealthy forms of introspection. Rather, healing prayers lead us to become more aware of dysfunction in our present lives and then connect that dysfunction with wounds we have experienced in our past stories. Thus healing prayers move us from our present into our past so that we can live positively and redemptively into our future. In this ministry, we do not get hung up on or stuck in our past, but rather deal with the parts of our past that affect us negatively today. As we shall see, this is not about blame, nor about relishing our status as victims.

Some Christians struggle with the idea that past wounding, particularly in one's younger years, is not fully resolved when we come to faith in Christ. These Christians argue that the conversion experience brings spiritual healing to all aspects of the past, and so healing for past hurts is not necessary, because it already took place at the moment of conversion. They feel that coming back to these matters is counter-productive, as it rakes up the past in unhealthy ways while also demeaning the scope of conversion.

Yet this is a serious misreading of the biblical story, for it collapses the lifelong journey of sanctification into one's justification by faith in Christ's finished work on the cross. When we come to faith, we move from being alienated from God to being embraced and welcomed home by God. But then we are called into the lifelong journey of growing into greater conformity to Christ. In this transformational process, we will need to deal with both present and past issues. Paul describes this process as putting away the old and embracing the new. He says:

> You were taught to put away your former way of life, your old self, corrupt and deluded by its lusts, and to be renewed in the spirit of your minds, and to clothe yourselves with the new self, created according to the likeness of God in true righteousness and holiness.   (Ephesians 4.22–24)

Similarly, in Colossians, he speaks of seeking the new, setting our minds on the new, putting to death the old, and getting rid of things that should no longer be a part of our new life in Christ (Colossians 3.1–11).

Because Paul addresses these epistles to Christians, the implication is that by the help of God's Spirit, we have a work of recovery to do *after* conversion. Clearly, brothers and sisters in the faith, as assistants to the Holy Spirit, can play a part in helping us to move beyond the things that still bind, oppress and distract us as we seek to grow in the Christian virtues and in Christlikeness.

In our case study, James was involved in this work of recovery. He had never faced his past wounding and abuse by his family, but had taken the blame for his suicidal thoughts upon himself. When he began to realize how his past hurts were affecting him in the present, he was drawn to seek healing. Though James had recounted to me the story of his wounding as a teenager, he still needed to be prepared for healing prayers.

Following is a general prayer that might open the preparation time for someone seeking healing like James.

୫୦୦୪

Holy One,

we recognize that your Spirit has moved through time and events to prepare this moment for James. As we listen together to discern where you are leading him and how you want to work your healing in his life, we ask that you grow his confidence and trust in your abiding love for him. By your gentle Spirit, draw him into the surety of your peace. Comfort him with your safe and loving presence and remind him that even though he may feel blind as he walks along the unknown path before him, you will never leave him nor forsake him.

Thank you that you have been carrying him and will continue to hold him and guide him throughout the days to come. Amen.

୫୦୦୪

General preparation guidelines

Preparatory discernment

In the following section, we outline general preparation procedures that are appropriate for those seeking healing prayers. To begin, one of the prayer team members schedules a time to meet with the person coming for ministry. This meeting will determine if a person is ready to proceed to healing prayers, or if he or she should receive some other form of ministry intervention.

In discerning whether or not a person should proceed, it is important to remember that not everyone needs inner-healing prayers at a particular time. Some may be better served by other forms of help. For example, if someone appears to have an underlying illness, the first step might be to recommend some form of psychological assessment. Or if someone is already on psychiatric medication, the prayer team will need to consider how the medication might impact the actual prayer ministry time. If there is deep wounding or oppression and the counsellee is pregnant, inner-healing prayers might be traumatic for the unborn child, and so it might be necessary to delay the inner-healing ministry time. Those who have a general sense of being unwell, but can't identify more specific hurts, may not yet be ready to receive inner-healing prayer.

Obviously, it is important for the discernment to be guided by the work and gifts of the Holy Spirit. Yet it is also important for the discernment to be guided by the professional wisdom and skills of trained members of a multidisciplinary prayer team, which might need to include the expertise of a medical doctor or a psychologist/psychiatrist or a social worker, along with those who are experienced in praying for inner healing. We should not drive a hard wedge between human wisdom based on professional training and the leading of the Spirit, as long as everything is framed in prayer.

If it becomes clear that a person would be best served by some other form of intervention, then an appropriate referral will need to be made. Such referrals should be made in the confidence that there are many paths to healing, and both medical and spiritual strategies are part of God's good purposes for a particular person. The prayer team might also decide to maintain contact with the counsellee to reconsider healing prayers in the future.

After making a referral for other forms of intervention, it is important to close the discernment time with a prayer for the counsellee's healing journey. Following are two examples of closing prayers that we might have used for James if we had decided that he was not yet ready for healing prayers.

ॐ

Jesus,

thank you for your guidance as we have gathered to discern the next steps for James. You are a God who uses many hands to heal, and we are grateful for everyone who surrounds James. We ask you to bless him as he meets with his doctor. Help him not to be afraid. Give him courage and trust that you will care for him through his doctor's skill and experience. Amen.

ဆာ၄၃

Jesus,

thank you for the work of healing that you have begun in James. We pray that you would bless his doctor with discernment and wisdom. We place James's story into your loving hands and ask you to remind us to watch and wait for your Spirit's guidance in his life. May your Spirit move before him as a light, guiding him along the straight way. May your Spirit surround him as a guard, protecting him and accompanying him. May your Spirit hover above him and beneath him, wrapping him in your mercy and grace. Amen.

ဆာ၄၃

If inner-healing prayer needs to be delayed because of pregnancy, a prayer such as the following might be used.

ဆာ၄၃

Dear Jesus,

you who are well acquainted with sorrow and grief, your tender heart knows of the deep burden that *N* . . . carries. We ask you to come with your Spirit to hold her story and carry it, just as she carries the life of this growing child in her body. In the same way that she nourishes the life of her baby and keeps that life growing and safe within her own flesh, reveal to her how you carry her within your heart and will sustain her and keep her safe until she is free within her body, mind and spirit to face this sorrow.

When her sorrow might affect the well-being of her baby, we ask your shield to protect this beautiful life, for your promised mercy extends to the descendants of all who turn to you. Bless both baby and mother with a growing awareness of your loving presence in all the places of their story.

You who long to cradle the sorrowing and vulnerable, we watch and wait for the signs of your care and provision for this mother and her child. We trust that your goodness and grace will be sufficient for them, because you have come to bring good news to the poor, to proclaim release to the captives and recovery of sight to the blind, to let the oppressed go free. In *N* . . .'s places of mourning, anoint her with the oil of gladness. When her spirit feels faint, give her a mantle of praise. Continue to complete your work in these two dear ones, whom we trust into your loving arms. Amen.

ℰℭ

Preparing for the healing ministry time

With James, it is fairly clear that healing prayers will be appropriate, as he does not appear to be suffering from a psychological illness. Moreover, he is on a transformational journey and is open to the Spirit's intervention in his life. Furthermore, he believes that healing prayers are appropriate.

Because James is proceeding with healing prayers, the next step is to explain what will take place during his inner-healing ministry time. It is very important for the counsellee to understand the key elements of the ministry of inner-healing prayer, as this lays the groundwork for the healing ministry time that will follow.

We begin by asking James if he is comfortable having two people on the ministry team, both a woman and a man. We also ask him if he will retell his story of wounding and confess his sins aloud to God in the presence of the prayer team. Furthermore, we ask if he is comfortable with the laying on of hands or anointing with oil, or if one of us uses the *charismata* (gifts) of the Spirit during the ministry time, or if we pray prayers of deliverance (taking authority in Jesus' name over the forces of oppression in his life). These dimensions of the ministry time need prior discussion, because they may not be part of a person's normal church experience and could cause surprise or distress during the actual prayer time – which should obviously be avoided.

These matters will be discussed more fully in the chapters that outline the actual ministry time, but it is important to mention them here so that any areas of concern can be discussed during the preparation time. It is important for the focus of the actual ministry time to be on healing prayers, rather than processing concerns about whether or not certain forms of deliverance are appropriate for Christians, or whether or not Christians today can draw on the gifts of the Holy Spirit.

Those who are not comfortable with some of these elements might need to meet with the prayer team for further discussion, prayer and reading. Though the ministry team and the counsellee may not agree about everything, they need to be on the same page so that the ministry time will not be hindered by intellectual questions and concerns. Because those seeking healing prayers need to feel a sense of theological and personal safety, further reading on inner healing may be important. Those in the Anglican or Episcopalian tradition may want to read Anne White's *Healing Adventure*[1] or Jim Glennon's *Your Healing is Within You*[2] or Agnes Sanford's *The Healing Gifts of the Spirit*.[3] Those within the Roman Catholic tradition may be well served by Francis MacNutt's classic *Healing*[4] or Michael Scanlan's concise *Inner Healing*[5] or Leo Thomas and Jan Alkire's *Healing as a Parish Ministry: Mending Body, Mind, and Spirit*.[6] Those within the Pentecostal and Charismatic Renewal tradition may be helped by John Wimber's *Power Healing*[7] or Charles Kraft's *Deep Wounds, Deep Healing*.[8] Those within the mainstream Protestant tradition might want to read David Seamands' *Healing of Memories*[9] or Leanne Payne's *The Healing Presence*.[10]

This survey indicates that contemporary pastors and counsellors within all the different Christian denominational traditions have engaged in the healing ministry. One of our hopes in writing this book is that the healing ministry will be integrated into the life of diverse local churches – rather than mostly offered as special seminars apart from the local church context.

If the counsellee has a lot of questions regarding the biblical and practical bases for healing, further discussion may be necessary before proceeding with healing prayers. Thus the inner-healing ministry is not a quick-fix ministry, but rather one that involves a significant time commitment on the part of the ministry team and the person seeking healing prayer. But if a person has struggled for many years because of a past wounding, the slow journey towards wholeness and restoration is worth it – and also to be expected.

The ministry team may also assign a counsellee further homework to help him or her become more attentive to past wounding. The person might be asked to journal about a particular phase of his or her life, or to look at family photos, or to ask a sibling or parent about what happened in the family dynamic during a particular time. Or the person might be asked to pray to the Holy Spirit over several weeks, asking for light to be shed on other matters requiring healing prayer. This prayer is based on John's vision that the Spirit will convict of sin (John 16.8–9), will guide us into truth, including the truth about ourselves (John 16.13), and will bring things to our remembrance (John 14.25). The completion of homework may or may not call for another preparation session. Following is an example of a prayer for illumination from the Holy Spirit.

ॐ○੪

Spirit of God,

have mercy on me, because I am in need of your help as I seek healing. Soften my heart to receive you. As I ponder my story, open my ears to hear what you are saying. Clear my sight to see what you want to show me. Help me understand what you are teaching me. Prepare the way forward so that I can bring my burden to Jesus. Surround me with your grace that will lead me on.

ഇരുഗ

Final instructions and outcomes

This work of preparation guides the counsellee into an understanding of the inner-healing ministry and what to anticipate during the actual prayer time. Before gathering for the ministry time, the person will have completed some further reflective work in order to be able to share areas of wounding and difficulty. With the preparation work complete, the counsellee will hopefully feel positive about moving forward. Now a date can be set for the prayer time, ideally when the counsellee will not be tired or stressed. Then the counsellee can be invited to ask family, friends and a few members of the church to pray in preparation for the ministry time, as well as during and after the ministry time. This makes healing prayers a communal experience.

At the conclusion of this ministry preparation time, you might pray something like the following for James.

ഇരുഗ

Lord,

into your hands we place all that we have discussed. Thank you for making a way for James to move towards life, where in the past there seemed to be only isolation, separation or death. We invite your Spirit to brood over James and to continue your work of preparing him for this coming time of prayer.

Remind James that you are with him and that your Spirit has brought him to this safe place, where he can trust his story into your light. Give him the courage to name his hurt and to hope in the healing you offer.

We give to you the spoken and unspoken desires for healing, as well as the fears that might show themselves and threaten to overwhelm James. Over the next two weeks, surround him with your gentle care and speak to him of your love and faithfulness.

We ask you to go before us and prepare a place of goodness in this coming time of healing prayer. Strengthen our spiritual eyes to see the work you are already doing and will continue to do. Help us to wait for you, that we might be ready to receive the abundance of your healing and restoration for James – to the glory of your holy name. Amen.

ෂⓒൽ

Conclusion

Because healing prayers have to do with the healing and transformation of past hurts that continue to affect us in the present, we might think of this slow and deep ministry as 'spiritual heart surgery'. If those past hurts are not dealt with, but are continually suppressed and repressed over our life journeys, they will continue to shape our present behaviours in negative ways. As we live out of that wounding, it will continue to grow and accumulate other negative influences in our lives. For this reason, healing prayers need to minister to the web of negativity that has grown over time, and this calls for holistic healing.

Thus as we embark upon the healing journey, we will need to prepare ourselves well, even as we recognize that healing can only come from the God who in the Spirit draws near to us. The remainder of this book will outline the major phases of healing prayer.

4

Inner healing: opening prayers

———————•◦•———————

James's issues surfaced during general counselling. From that time of sharing, he acknowledged his need for healing prayers. During our preparation time, we introduced the framework for healing prayer so that he would know what to expect during the actual ministry time. After the preparation time, James began praying and completing his assigned homework. During this time, he gained further insight about what happened on that 'fatal' day and how those events were part of a much wider mosaic of dysfunction within his family.

When James comes to the prayer ministry time, it will be important for him to begin by sharing again his story of wounding and struggle. This way, he can share what emerged during his homework assignments, while also giving the team members who were not present during the preparation time a chance to listen prayerfully to his story.

Introduction

In this chapter on opening prayers, we will begin by describing the composition of the prayer team. Second, we will illustrate the kinds of prayers that the members of the prayer team have been praying between the preparation time and the actual ministry session. Third, we will offer examples of prayers that those who are supporting the counsellee might pray. Fourth, we will describe the healing prayer setting. Finally, we outline a format for prayers that might open the ministry time.

It is important to acknowledge here that even though a counsellee might understand the basic format for healing prayer, some experience tension and apprehension before the scheduled ministry time as they begin to wonder about what will actually happen. This is particularly true when a counsellee completes homework assignments and a fuller sense of wounding emerges. Those who open up their inner hurts to others often feel deep embarrassment, shame or fear, and it takes trust and courage to invite others to minister to them. Counsellees may also worry about what God will do during the ministry time. Will God heal? Will anything distressing happen?

Although inner healing follows patterns of prayer, it is not a stratified methodology. We are not begging from God, nor demanding something of God, nor shouting triumphantly at God. Rather, we humbly draw near to God's presence, and we attend to God's heart for the healing and restoration of humanity. Those involved in the prayer ministry seek God on behalf of someone who has been wounded by life. We are not drawing an absent or reluctant God into our daily concerns, but rather growing in friendship with the God who is always with us. Out of this confidence, we join with the good purposes of the One who seeks, reveals and heals.

Composition of the prayer team

The prayer team may consist of any combination of clergy and lay persons. This language of 'clergy' and 'lay' does not imply hierarchical distinctions, for all God's people are the *laos* of God. All are in Christ. All have the Spirit. All have spiritual gifts. All are called to service within and beyond the community of faith. Clergy have a particular, not a higher, calling.[1]

But ideally, if the team consists of lay persons alone, it should be an extension of a local church, or a Christian para-church organization, or accountable to the board of a healing ministry. We emphasize this because we think that the healing ministry should not be isolated from faith communities, but rather integrated into the pastoral ministry of any church. Healing is the outworking of the presence of Christ, through the Spirit, among the Church, which is his body. In this way, healing is a *communion* with the risen Christ.

Ideally, those who are part of healing prayer teams should be mature Christians who have experienced healing prayers themselves and who have had at least some training in this ministry. We offer inner healing and deliverance seminars at seminaries and colleges so that those who are training for the pastoral ministry or for lay ministry can have a biblical and theological basis for healing prayers. Though formal training in pastoral theology, spiritual direction, psychology or social work is often helpful for this ministry, we do not think it is necessarily essential. Anyone who is mature, loving and who understands the praxis of the healing ministry can be an effective practitioner. However, a ministry team will ideally consist of persons with a variety of life experiences, including at least one member with some formal training.

Though some healing ministry practitioners, such as Agnes Sanford, had a special calling for the healing ministry and special gifts of the Spirit, we do not think these are necessary. Some may not have a special calling, but simply a deep desire to bless others because they were blessed by healing prayers. Some may not sense that they have any special spiritual gifts, and yet those gifts might be given by the Spirit during the prayer time. Whether one has a special calling or not, this ministry must flow from grace, freedom and love. For the point is not about how gifted we are, but rather about looking to the God who heals. For this reason, the healing ministry of the Church needs to be recovered in our time.

We also believe that it is important for the prayer team to consist of both male and female members. First, we believe women and men have equal status and roles in the community of faith.[2] Second, we believe women and men with different life orientations and gifts make a richer team than those teams with only one gender. Finally, if someone has been wounded by his or her mother, the female team member is better suited to pray healing prayers in this area – and vice versa for the male.

Prayers of the prayer team

As we look at specific prayers for the period between the preparation time and the actual ministry session, we return to James's story.

The gap between when James first opened up his story of wounding until the actual ministry time is covered by many prayers. Our ministry team prays for James to be at peace during the prayer time and open to the work of the Spirit. We pray that we will all be prepared to receive with gratitude whatever God has to give James. We pray that God will give James deeper insights about the nature of his wounding and his need for healing and restoration. We pray for prayer support during the actual ministry time, and we pray that we will be assistants to the Holy Spirit.

Following are three examples of prayers we might pray as we prepare ourselves for the ministry time. The first two might be prayed by those who will not hear James's story until the ministry time, whereas the third example reflects a prayer from the team member who met with James and heard his story ahead of time.

ঝ০৫

Holy One,

as I wait and watch for your healing, I am so aware that you are other than I am. You have the strength to carry what I cannot. You remain present when I turn away in fear. Your powerful love brings forth life, yet my knowledge of your love is so small.

I long for you to fill me with your holy yearning for the healing of nations. Cleanse me and work in me to restore your people. Show me your reconciling ways. Teach me your paths of peace. Lead me by your light of faith.

Come, Holy One, prepare me to be your handmaiden. I offer you all the concerns and brokenness of my own life, all my abilities and weaknesses, my very self. May your kingdom come, your will be done here, as it is in heaven. Amen.

ঝ০৫

Spirit of God,

I lift up James and ask you to encourage him as he moves towards you. Please give him what he needs today and surprise him with a sense of your peace, which is not limited by understanding. May this peace be a foretaste of all that you have for him.

Holy Spirit, I ask you to attend to James where he feels fear or rejection, silence or neglect. You are the mighty warrior who does not sleep, but prays on our behalf day and night with groans too deep for words. Move into the darkest places of James's night and lead him to the light of morning.

Lord, I don't know how our prayer time with James will be, but I trust your ways. It is your time. Be present to all who are part of this healing journey. Amen.

ℰℭ

Jesus,

it is painful to hear James's story. His burden is too heavy for me. I taste the bitterness of his wounds.

Yet I hear the hope James has in you. I see the steps of faith he has made in preparing for this prayer time. I know he wants to entrust you with his wounding. Guide him in his remembrance, so that his healing may be deep and full. Your Spirit has gently led him to this place, and I trust that you will restore James and guide him along the path of life.

Come, Lord Jesus. Come. By your power, heal his story and transform his life. Fulfil your desire and purpose in James. Thank you that this is your work, and this is your will. You have already overcome, and I look forward to seeing what you will do for James. Amen.

ℰℭ

Additional prayer support

Because we are called to be a community in Christ, we recommend organizing further prayer support for the ministry healing time. Both the counsellee and the prayer team will be encouraged by knowing that others are joining in prayer for God's freedom and wholeness to come.

The prayer team might organize some of this support from those who have an understanding of this ministry or have received healing prayers in the past, as they will know how to pray specifically. This support team could gather in an adjacent room to where the healing prayers take place.

The counsellee could also organize friends, persons from the church and others to pray during the ministry time – either on site or at home. Choosing one's own prayer support is empowering and gives one a sense of solidarity with family and/or friends. Sometimes, those who participate in healing prayer as part of a prayer support team are then led to seek healing prayers for themselves in the future.

Following is an example of a prayer that family members, friends or church members who are part of a healing prayer support team might pray for the person they want to see blessed and healed.

℘CЗ

Lord,

bless James with your strong assurance and gentle presence. Soften his heart so that he can receive your healing and restoration. Open his eyes to see himself as you see him and as you have created him to be. Help him to see you as you are so that he can lean into the expectation of what you will do.

Bless and prepare the prayer team to engage with you and with your child, James, and with each other. Strengthen them and place your guard around them and around the prayer time and space. May your truth push back anything that would overwhelm them.

Sustain those of us who are interceding for James. Lead us into your heart for James so that we can pray in accordance with your Spirit. Help us to trust and not grow weary as we watch and wait for the coming of your mercy and comfort. Open us to receive your Spirit, who prays within us as we look to you. Amen.

൲൝

The setting for prayer

Over the years, I have prayed healing prayers with others in retreat centres, in homes or churches with consecrated prayer rooms, and in my study at the various places where I taught. Mary and I often prayed in my study at Regent College, but always at night, when the building was quiet and there were not masses of students milling around. It is important for those in the Protestant tradition to think carefully about sacred spaces, for it is deeply significant to pray for others in a place that has heard the prayers and cries of God's people over many years.

Thus the setting for the healing ministry time is important, and we need to prepare it thoughtfully. Healing prayers cannot be held in an old, dingy church hall, but need to take place in a roomy, uncluttered and aesthetically pleasing space. Ideally, the setting will include appropriate symbolism, such as a bowl of water for washing hands to depict forgiveness and cleansing, a vessel with oil for anointing, a Christ candle to depict the light of God's presence. Such symbols must be sensitive to the story and experience of the person coming for prayer. Most importantly, the setting must be free from distractions and interruptions, including phones. Thus the space should convey comfort, peace and welcome.

Prayer team members should gather shortly before the appointed time. As they wait for the counsellee to arrive, they might pray a prayer for the room, such as the following.

൲൝

Holy One,

come and consecrate this space as holy. As we gather and wait, come into each corner and cleanse and prepare it for your spacious presence. Mark and guard this room for your ministry so that it reflects your wide embrace of love for James. We ask you to lift from our shoulders the concerns we have carried here, so that we might be free to attend to your Spirit's movement within James. We welcome you. We rest in you. We bless your name.

Jesus, as we gather and wait for James, we invite you to be our companion. Guide us along the path you have walked before us, so that James can receive what he needs by your hand. Cleanse and strengthen us for all that you want to do in us and through us. Enlarge our spirits to receive and know your heart for James. Fill us with your love for him, your passion to heal him, your longing to bless him.

Holy Spirit, be with James as he journeys here. Calm his fears and comfort him as he arrives. Give him courage to step on to the unknown path of freedom you have stretched before him. Into his spirit, breathe your life-giving hope. Amen.

ଧଓଃ

Our God,

thank you for this space, which has been set aside for the purpose of healing. Into this space, we invite your hospitable love and healing comfort. Like the fragrance of morning, bless this space with your presence. Fill each corner and object with your grace. May your Spirit attend to James's spirit, body, mind and emotions as he approaches this time. As he walks into this room, may he feel your peaceable mercy. May your light mark the edges of this healing time and space, guarding us from distractions and disturbances. May your rest hold James so that he feels safe. Make this place a home for your spacious love in Jesus' name. Amen.

ଧଓଃ

Opening prayers

As we move into our discussion of the opening prayers during the ministry session, we return to James's story and our role as his prayer team.

Once James is welcomed into the room and feels comfortable, the prayer team gently guides him into the ministry time with opening prayers. These opening prayers touch on several themes. First, we thank God for James's journey towards healing. Second, we ask the Spirit to be present and to lead the prayer time, bringing us unity of heart and purpose. Third, we ask for God's protection over everyone in the room and over our loved ones. Fourth, we ask for the gifts of the Spirit to be given during the ministry time.

In these comprehensive opening prayers, we anticipate God's presence as healer, protector, empowerer and giver of the Spirit's gifts. We do not need to coerce God, or 'psych up' one another as a prayer team, or make promises to James about what God will do. Rather, we enter this prayer time as faithful seekers who have witnessed what God has already done with gratitude, and therefore we trust in what God will continue to do. In this posture of peaceful anticipation, we quietly hope in the God who has drawn near in Christ and will come again in this setting through his life-giving Spirit.

Following are two examples of opening prayers for a prayer team.

&OCG

God,

your prophet Isaiah promised that one day we would no longer lean on the one who struck us, but on the Holy One in truth. Through Jesus and the Holy Spirit, you have made a way for us to lean on you. We thank you for the hope of leaning on you together during this time and ask you to come and bless James. Keep him safe within your powerful love. Protect him from confusion and fear. Clarify his words and thoughts as he shares his heart with you.

May your light surround this space and time and guard against any distractions or disruptions to your work. Watch over our loved ones as we pray. Bless those who are praying for this time with insight into your heart for James.

Prepare us to receive your grace and mercy. Cleanse us from all that would be a barrier to you. Attune our ears to hear your voice and to listen to one another. May we be one, as you are One: Father, Son and Holy Spirit. Strengthen all of us to pray in your Spirit and entrust us with the gifts you would give to make your way known. We wait on you and are willing to receive whatever you offer during this time.

Spirit of God, you come with healing in your wings. Move into the story that James gives you with your cleansing love. Restore each hidden and hurting moment with your healing presence. In the name of Jesus our Saviour. Amen.

ᚼᚩᚳᚱ

Lord Jesus,

thank you for your brooding Spirit, which does not sleep, but hovers over us with groans and prayers too deep for words. Thank you for rising to meet James in his story and for guiding him to this safe place. Thank you for your faithful presence in his life.

We invite you to come with your healing hands, your comforting presence and your loving guidance. We give you this time and space and ask you to place your guard around us, pushing back anything that would disrupt your good work here. Look after all who are praying and those whom we love, near or far, so that we can attend to you.

We give you the concerns and events of our day, so that we can hear your voice and join in your mending work for James. We ask you for the gifts of faith and discernment and any other gifts we might need as we pray. These we will receive with thanksgiving. Help us to see with the light of your truth and to feel with your heart of compassion. Help us to listen well to one another and to follow the guidance of your Holy Spirit.

Spirit of God, you come with healing in your wings. Bless James with your love and comfort him with your peace. Draw him into your gentle presence as he names the tender things of his life. We welcome you. We bless your name. We give you thanks. Amen.

ᛒᏟᏟᏰ

As part of the opening prayers, James is also invited to pray. Following are two examples of such opening prayers for James.

ᛒᏟᏟᏰ

Lord,

I come ready to open to you the parts of my life that need your healing power. I am afraid, but I trust that you have brought me here. I want you to heal me. I need you to heal me. I no longer want to live outside the reach of your love and transforming power. Please come. Help me be honest. Help me believe that you will listen and respond. Help me hope that you have something new for me. Thank you for those who have gathered here around me. Through them, I know that you are with me, and I am not alone. Be with us all. In Jesus' name. Amen.

ᛒᏟᏟᏰ

Jesus,

thank you for this place and for this time to pray. Please guide my words and thoughts as I let go of this hurt. Help me to receive your love and the gifts you have to give me. You have given me hope through those who are surrounding me, and I want to entrust you with what is deep in my heart. I am afraid, but I ask you to be with me and with those who are praying for me. I am so grateful that I can be honest with you and say, I believe, help my unbelief! Help me to open my heart to you. Help me to forgive. Come, Lord Jesus. Come and heal me. Amen.

ℰℭ

Conclusion

In this chapter, we have discussed several issues regarding the composition of the prayer team, the value of prayer support, the setting for the prayer time, and the nature of the opening prayers during the actual ministry time.

From all that we have learned, it is hardly surprising that the ministry of inner healing has also been called prayer counselling. Yet we prefer the phrase healing prayers, since prayer – rather than counselling – is the primary focus.

Prayer is the heartbeat of the healing ministry. And since prayer rightly defines our relationship to God, prayer is the royal highway to the open heart of God.

5

Listening time: prayers of discernment

After the opening prayers, the inner-healing session moves to the listening time, where James has the opportunity to retell and expand on his story of wounding and struggle as it relates to his desire to receive healing prayers. This retelling is important for several reasons. First, any prayer team members who were not present during the preparation time have not heard his story. Second, after James acknowledged his wounding, he completed the preparation session, read about inner healing and spent additional time in reflection and prayer. Thus his story may have expanded, and he may have gained deeper insights into his hurts, grief and loss. During this time, he may have also grown in his knowledge that God will draw near and come to his aid. As James shares his story, the team listens to the voice of the Spirit, who guides the time of prayer.

Introduction

In this chapter, we will explain why the listening time is so important. We will then give some guidelines about how to conduct this time, and finally we will discuss the value and nature of discernment prayers.

When we listen well to others, we offer them a rare and precious gift, particularly if they are hurting and seeking help. In our contemporary world, people are so involved in personal externalization and seeking iconic status that they make much time for talking, but little space for listening. Because we are so self-preoccupied, we quickly move from half-hearted listening to talking about what concerns us. But in the healing prayer setting, we need to lay aside our own concerns and give all of our regard to the other person. Listening has a sacramental power, and in the ministry of healing prayer, it is also a spiritual gift – for at its heart, listening is all about discernment.

There is also growing evidence that listening well to another person has healing properties. Dr Curt Thompson explains:

> When a person tells her story and is truly heard and under-stood, both she and the listener undergo actual changes in their brain circuitry. They feel a greater sense of emotional and relational connection, decreased anxiety, and greater awareness of and compassion for others' suffering.[1]

The value of the listening time

When we listen to another person's story with respect, sensitivity and discernment, we enter into the healing journey. As we see with James, everything that has taken place so far has been part of his healing and recovery, for healing prayers involve a complex set of interventions rather than one singular 'fix'. Thus the whole process – the preparation, the healing prayer time, the pastoral follow-up – helps a person on the road towards wholeness.

Usually, those who seek healing prayers have hidden or repressed their stories of wounding within the darkest and deepest recesses of their memories. Because these stories have never been fully acknowledged, let alone told, the memories often shock and em-barrass those who finally face what they have been burying for so long. As a consequence, many people who come for healing prayer often feel incredibly vulnerable.

Others, however, can tell you their stories of pain almost with-out taking a breath. Though their stories might be more evident, immediate and well known, they are stuck in a rut because they have not experienced any forward movement towards true free-dom. The pain of these stories is often dressed in hopelessness, despair, rationalization and self-pity. For some, the story of their abuse may have become their persona.

When we tell our stories in a setting of respect, hopefulness and prayer, we experience freedom and healing. One often hears a counsellee say, 'It is such a relief to finally get this story out into the open.' Or, 'I never thought I would find the courage to tell my story.' Or, 'I never imagined I would find people with whom my story would be safe.'

When we open up stories of wounding within the setting of healing prayers, we open these stories to God. In this setting, as members of the prayer team, we become 'representatives' of the body of Christ. In this way, healing prayers differ from general pastoral and psychological counselling. For in these professions, one opens one's issues and concerns to the competencies and skills of a professional. Yet in the ministry of inner healing, though some may be professionally trained, our role is to pray as fellow travellers. We have sat where the counsellee now sits, and we are continuing along the road of our own healing journeys. As members of the community of faith, we seek the God who seeks us out in Christ. We look to Christ to make us whole and to the Spirit to guide us in this process. Thus we feel vulnerable[2] rather than competent and confident. And we come into the healing prayer setting with faith, hope and love rather than with certainty.

The dynamics of the listening time

We must recognize that people tell their stories differently. Some will 'gush' it out. Others will tell it hesitantly. Some will need patient, gentle help in staying focused. Others will get stuck and be unable to proceed. Some will cry as they tell their story. Others will express undercurrents of anger and bitterness. Still others will appear flippant as they recount their familiar tale of woe.

Because everyone is different, each will need the freedom to share in different ways. For this reason, we will need to be aware of our own communication styles so that we don't expect others to communicate in the same way. For example, I tend to be very concise and logical in the way I communicate, but I must not expect that of others. Mary is much more fluid in her communication style and so can connect better with the counsellee who happily wanders in his or her storytelling. So we must be patient and create an open, spacious atmosphere for the counsellee. The storytelling time should not be rushed, as it is a slow, unfolding journey.

Generally, we should not interrupt the storyteller, except to clarify when there is confusion, offer assurance when there is hesitancy, and give comfort when there is emotional distress. We are present to listen well, and this involves prayer. Thus we are prayerfully listening.

Prayers of discernment for James

As we listen to James tell his story, we pray silently, 'lifting' him into God's presence and asking the Spirit to give us wisdom so that we can make sense of his narrative and understand the impact his wounding has had on his life. At the same time, we seek to discern the key themes – or the heartbeat – of his story. Listening well is a hermeneutic strategy, an exercise in interpretation, an exegesis of the 'text'.[3] As we listen to James's story, we discern the critical areas for prayer. What are the deeper issues of wounding, and which are more peripheral? What is being said and what is being left unsaid?

As James tells his story, he talks constantly about his father's attitudes, words and behaviours. But he does not mention his mother. This strikes some of us as 'strange' and as something that needs to be addressed at some point. Throughout the listening time, we inwardly pray some of the following prayers. These silent prayers form an inner dialogue with God as we listen to James. They are prayers of the moment and are not meant to distract us from listening.

$$\infty \text{\Large \omega}$$

Jesus, have mercy on us, sinners saved by your grace.

Jesus, I feel your heart for James. Thank you for your love and compassion.

Lord, we wait for you to heal. Go ahead of us and prepare the way.

I am open to you in this story. Help me to hear what you are saying to James. Help me to know what you are desiring for him.

Open this story with your grace and mercy. Reveal your truth to James. Bless him in this moment.

Lord, what is behind his words? What is his posture saying?

Jesus, help me to hear what James is trying to say. Give me an ear to recognize what is held in silence. Help me to notice the 'hidden moments' that may reveal something more.

Holy Spirit, show me what causes James to respond in this way.

God, I feel this hurt deeply within my spirit and my body. I give you my anger (shock, sadness, own memories etc.). Take it and keep it for me while I am listening to James. Don't let it distract me.

Lord, what is important here?

Lord, what is true in this? What do you want me to hear?

Spirit of God, there is silence about James's mother. Shine your light and gently make space for that part of his story.

I give you this question as a prayer. Expand it in James and show us what to do with it.

Spirit of God, illuminate the words that you want to respond to in this story. Help us to see them clearly and to hear them well.

God, help me to remember, so that I can pray through this story well.

Jesus, how do you feel about this? How do you respond?

Holy One, remind me of your character as I listen – your holy anger, your forgiveness, your grace.

☜❦☞

Sometimes, we may need to pray silently during the listening time for a pushing back of the powers and principalities that seek to thwart the telling of the story. We may sense this when a counsellee seems afraid or unable to tell certain parts of his or her story. Or we may pray this way when the counsellee exhibits feelings of despair and hopelessness, or when there is an emotional response that causes distress.

When we sense these things during our prayer time for James, we pray that the Spirit of God will continue to provide a safe place for James to continue with his story. Following are some examples of these inward prayers.

8003

Lord, give me an awareness of how the evil one is working in this story.

Lord, guard James in his anger so that he may speak to you about what was not right. Thank you that it will not overcome him, for you can handle it.

Jesus, by your name and authority, I place your power to heal between James and all that is giving him discomfort and distress in this moment.

Comforter, come close to James and give him strength. Assure him of your love as he speaks about this sorrow and pain.

Thank you that you are providing a safe place. Remind James of your care.

Jesus, expose and break the power of any lie that is binding or threatening James in this telling.

Holy One, give James the courage to name his fears so that they lose their power. Replace them with your love.

In the name of the Lord Jesus Christ, I declare that this story, this space, and this time are held within the living power of Jesus' blood shed on the cross. All that seeks to threaten or dismay, stand back.

As a child of God, I hold the keys of the kingdom, and in the authority of Jesus' death and resurrection, I bind the presence and power of all that would threaten James. In the name of the Lord Jesus Christ, I command you to be still.

8003

Conclusion

In this chapter, we highlighted the value and importance of the listening time. Telling one's story, particularly a story of difficulty and pain, is a freeing process that brings one out of darkness and into the light. This breaks the power of unacknowledged or suppressed things in our lives, which often accumulate 'powers' that are disproportionate to the actual events. Darkness tends to swirl around these hidden wounds, giving the evil one a foothold that causes distress. Disclosure begins the liberating and healing process.

We also emphasized that our listening needs to be respectful. This is not a time to give advice or counselling. Rather, we offer ourselves to prayerful discernment. The discernment provides the basis for the actual healing prayers, when we will traverse the themes of James's story more fully. When we begin to offer healing prayers, the Holy Spirit will need to help us with the gift of remembrance. For as members of the ministry team, we are praying and listening at the same time. While offering James's story up to God, we ask God to give us wisdom in making sense of his story so that we can pray appropriately for his healing and well-being.

6

Prayers of confession and repentance

———◆•◆•◆———

After the listening and discerning time, we consider prayerfully how to respond to James's story. Even though the prayer team may have some clear ideas about how to proceed, it is critical for James to be on the same page. Because healing prayers are communal and co-operative, it is important to come alongside James as a fellow traveller and agree together about the best way forward. We don't 'do' these prayers to James. Rather, we empower him and guide him into the basic framework for healing prayers. Thus we might begin by asking James some questions, such as, 'Where do we start with further healing prayers?' 'What are the key themes that need attention?'

As we prepare to respond to James's story, one of our central concerns will be whether James is working with a blame mentality (for example, my father has messed up my life), or if he understands his wounding more broadly. In accompanying James into healing prayers, we might recognize that what his father did was totally inexcusable, yet also acknowledge his father as a wounded person. Furthermore, James might need space to acknowledge his own sins of reaction. Over the years, he might have lived with hatred and bitterness towards his dad. Because of this bitterness, he might have 'hit back' at his father or others in various ways.

Introduction

In this chapter, we discuss prayers of confession and repentance. In these prayers, we neither blame nor excuse the perpetrator, but begin by acknowledging our own sins of reaction. Prayers for repentance usually fall at the beginning of the healing prayer framework, since most counsellees have harboured anger, bitterness and even hatred towards the ones who have wounded them. Though this is an understandable reaction, the Gospels call Christians to forgive and not to hate (Luke 6.37–38; 18.35), because hateful retaliation does not heal us, but brings further hurt to ourselves and others. Moreover, the Lord's Prayer teaches us to seek forgiveness for our sins before we try to forgive others' sins against us (Matthew 6.12). In this way, repentance becomes the royal highway to freedom and healing. For when there is the grace of repentance, the kingdom or reign of God breaks into our lives (Mark 1.14–15).

From a psychological point of view, when we bring something into the open, we become free. Carl Jung says that 'every personal secret acts as a sin and a fault'. He continues that when something is not brought to the light, 'it breaks free from the conscious to become an autonomous complex' and begins to take on 'a kind of separate existence'. For this reason, he says, 'a secret shared can be fruitful'.[1]

Yet in many cases, counsellees are not ready to think about their sins of reaction, because they have been focusing for so long on their wounding. This focus may be so dominant that the counsellee is unable to say prayers of forgiveness for those who hurt them. As a result, we may need to begin the healing time with prayers of separation that 'cut' the emotional bondage between the wounder and wounded (or victim and perpetrator). Or if a counsellee is 'stuck' in patterns of hatred and unforgiveness towards the person who hurt him or her, we may need to begin with prayers of deliverance. In such cases, we will later need to circle back around to prayers of confession, repentance and forgiveness.

The grace of repentance

In the *Catechism of the Catholic Church*, the 'sacrament of penance and reconciliation'[2] is located under the broader heading of 'The Sacraments of Healing'.[3] Thus in the Roman Catholic tradition (as well as in Eastern Orthodox Christianity), confession and repentance are linked to God's healing presence in one's life. To put that more strongly, one could say that confession is a healing process, for it brings into the light of God's grace the things we have been holding on to or hiding. Because unrecognized or unrepentant sins in our lives remain hidden – and often active – within us, they can block or stranglehold God's free movement of grace in our lives. But when we confess our sins, we open a space for God's healing and renewing work within us.

Within the Anglican or Episcopalian tradition, confessional practices are also placed within the context of the healing ministry. The 1549 Prayer Book (along with the 1927–8 revision) speaks of the role of confession and absolution as integral to the healing ministry.[4] Within this framework, confession of sin is identified as the in-breaking of the kingdom of God, and the coming of Jesus Christ through the Spirit is a healing and renewing presence. The Book of Common Prayer includes a section on the rite of 'The Reconciliation of a Penitent', which says:

> I confess to Almighty God, to his Church, and to you, that I have sinned by my own fault in thought, word, and deed, in things done and left undone; especially _____
> [the person making this confession is invited here to be specific about sins committed]. For these and all other sins . . . I am truly sorry. I pray [for] God to have mercy on me.

After this prayer of confession, the following absolution is used:

> Our Lord Jesus Christ, who has left power to his Church to absolve all sinners, who truly repent and believe in him, of his great mercy forgive you all your offenses; and by his authority committed to me, I absolve you from all your sins. In the name of the Father, and of the Son, and of the Holy Spirit. Amen.[5]

While the framework implies that the confession is being made to an ordained member of the clergy, there is no reason that such authority could not be delegated to lay persons who are exercising this pastoral ministry on behalf of the Church in the name of Christ.

Agnes Sanford, who is part of the Anglican/Episcopalian tradition, speaks of how the 'swing-up into joy and power' is as important as 'the swing-down into repentance'.[6] She notes that repentance 'begins with being sorry for our sins, but it ends with joy, because it ends with a changed life'.[7] Thus the healing presence of God can come to us through the confessional and through the service of Holy Communion.[8]

Even within Protestantism, the Reformers allowed for the practice of confession, though they rejected the meritorious and obligatory nature of confession to a member of the clergy or to a fellow believer. In John Calvin's *Institutes*, he says that 'having made his [her] confession to God, the sinner confesses voluntarily to man'. He continues that if a person confessing to God finds herself or 'himself distressed in heart' because of the nature of her or his sins, then such a person 'can unburden himself . . . to his pastor in order to receive consolation'.[9]

In *Life Together*, Dietrich Bonhoeffer, a German theologian and martyr, makes a strong case for us to confess our sins to another, pointing out that this is 'the profoundest kind of humiliation',[10] as it requires that we become open about our failures. But it also means that 'the last stronghold of self-justification is abandoned',[11] and an internal power is broken in our lives. While Bonhoeffer does not link confession specifically to healing, he does identify it as a great grace. He writes, 'So in the Christian community, when the call to brotherly confession and forgiveness goes forth, it is a call to the great grace of God in the church.'[12]

Yet we need to realize that Bonhoeffer's practice of mutual confession is not a normal practice within mainstream Protestantism and Evangelicalism. The Reformation tradition is clear that we do not need any intermediaries between ourselves and God. Because Christ is the mediator, we may come directly to Christ with our sins and needs. This flows from the key Reformation teaching that 'all believers . . . share in the ministry and mission of our Lord Jesus Christ through the charisms that they have received'.[13] However, the Reformation tradition also allows for the role of clergy, since 'all do not share in the pastoral ministry of the church'.[14] Since the pastoral ministry involves the administration of word and sacrament, we need to recover a vision of the healing dimensions of word and sacrament – including confession and absolution – as part of the pastoral ministry and as part of the whole people of God in exercising the various gifts of the Spirit.

Moreover, Bonhoeffer's concept of mutual confession does not create intermediaries between ourselves and God, but rather builds authentic Christian community. Such a community is built not simply on the sharing of gifts and strengths, but also on sharing our weaknesses and sins. In the ministry of healing prayers, the focus is on confession of sin to God in the presence of brothers and sisters in the faith who can proclaim God's forgiveness. This practice can be exercised by clergy and laity alike.

James's prayer of repentance

Fortunately, James is willing and happy to start with prayers of repentance. He recognizes that he not only turned his wounding against himself in the form of self-harm, but he also turned it against his father. James hated and rejected his father, just as his father rejected and wounded James.

At this point in the healing ministry time, James is encouraged to confess to God, in the presence of the prayer team members, his sins of reaction to his father's mistreatment. In praying this prayer, James has to find his own words. Some may pray very briefly, whereas others may pray more expansively. Following is an example of what James's prayer of confession in relation to his dad might look like.

૪૦૯૩

Jesus,

I need to tell you these things, to bring them to the light. Please help me to remember and to speak honestly. I confess that I have believed my father. I have agreed with him when he said that I was no good, that I was not a 'real man'. Every time I tried to be a 'real man' I failed, just like that day in the paddock. I could not keep running. I could not win the races. I could not keep up with my team. I could not give Dad what he wanted – a good son. I believed that I was a worthless failure and would never change. I was angry with myself that I could not please my father, even though I tried. Ever since that day, I have felt worthless and angry, blaming myself and wondering why I should keep trying. I continue to judge and reject myself. I am still angry. I continue to hate myself, and I think that when others get to know me, they should hate me, too. I have thought of killing myself, and I have even wondered if committing suicide would finally please my dad. I find it very hard to admit this out loud – Lord, have mercy.

Jesus, I have hated my father for judging and rejecting me. I have believed that I have the right to judge him. Because he failed to love and accept me, I have refused to give him my love. I have tried to get away from him and to quell my desire to please him. Jesus, help me to be honest. I am angry and bitter that I still long for his love, and I have held that against him and myself. I have pushed down my feelings and walked away from him. When I have hurt him, I have felt justified. I have worked so hard not to 'need' my father and to pay him back, to give him what he deserves.

And you did not help me when I was young, so why should I trust you now? I have been angry with you for making me this way. I have blamed you for doing such a rotten job of making me. I have thought that you were just like my father – and I believed you saw me as I saw myself.

But you have not rejected me. You have wooed me, accepted me and loved me. I hear you inviting me to give my feelings and justifications to you. I have been tied up and weighed down with all this anger and bitterness for so long that I am afraid of letting it go. Yet I can no longer live with it, and I do not want to carry it any longer. I am tired of hating and rejecting myself and my father. I feel exposed and vulnerable, and I long to experience your freedom and love.

I feel like I am in a deep, dark place, but I am looking at your light. I choose to trust you. I give you these feelings. Forgive

me for my anger, my hatred and my bitterness towards my
father, towards myself and towards you. I give you my silence
and rejection of my father, myself and others and ask you to
forgive me. Forgive me for wanting and trying to kill myself.
Please release me from these heavy burdens and heal me. I
need you. I cast myself on your mercy. Amen.

℘℃ℨ

Because James has carried his anger and bitterness towards his
father for so long, praying this powerful confession is a moving
and emotional experience. When James finishes his confession,
one of the team members prays, reflecting God's grace and love
back to James, reminding him that all who turn to Christ in faith
and repentance receive forgiveness and healing through the power
of Christ's resurrection. The following prayer is an example of
an absolution that might be prayed for James by one of the team
members.

℘℃ℨ

Quickly, quickly, you come, Righteous God, over whom darkness
and sin have no power. Through the storm of emotion and
burden, the weight of sorrow and bitterness, fear and hatred,
you have heard James. You honour his honesty, and you hear
his cry for help. Because you are true to your promise that all
who humble themselves and turn towards you in repentance
will be saved and healed, so you extend your hand to James,
seeking to rescue and restore him.

James, because of God's mercy, I declare that by the living
power and strong authority of Jesus Christ, your prayer has
been heard and you are forgiven. The Lord delights in your
turning away from these spoken sins of reaction against yourself,
your father and God. They have been received into his grace,
and they have been taken as far away from you as the east
is from the west – so far that they will never be yours to carry

again. The Lord delights in forgiving you. He rises to greet you, to release you from these burdens and to set your feet upon a rock in the land of the living. It is done. Amen.

This declarative absolution is important, for it is not based upon asking, but rather on proclaiming the heart of the gospel. This performative prayer declares God's forgiveness through Christ to James. As James embraces this good news, his burdens are lifted. As Bonhoeffer points out, 'Pastoral authority can be attained only by the servant of Jesus who seeks no power of his own, who himself is a brother among brothers submitted to the authority of the Word.'[15] And it is this brother or sister who acts towards us on Christ's behalf. This person 'hears the confession of our sins in Christ's stead and . . . forgives our sins in Christ's name'.[16]

Exploring further prayers of repentance with James

The role of the prayer team is difficult and challenging, for members need to be careful not to misread James's story by interpreting it through their own issues and judgements. Yet team members do need to interpret James's story and bring to light what might otherwise be hidden from view.

Throughout James's life, the focus of his wounding has been on the rejection and abuse he experienced from his father, whom James could never please because he never became 'a man' in his father's eyes. Even though James's mother was not the focus of his wounding, it is clear from James's story that she was in collusion with his father, for she did not confront her husband nor protect James. And on the night of that 'fatal' day, she was tragically absent. She did not enter James's room to comfort him or to give him something to eat or to see if he was okay.

Noting the mother's absence in the story, one of the prayer team members asks James about her. The question catches James by surprise, because he has not thought about her. Yet as James remembers his mother's role in his wounding, he begins to sob uncontrollably. Then he begins to talk about their relationship, praising her in many ways, but also acknowledging her fear of his father and her neglect of James as she sought to keep the peace.

At this point, James realizes that prayers of repentance in relation to his mother are also appropriate. He recognizes that he has despised his mother for her weakness and fear. He acknowledges that he has bitterly resented her failure to protect him from his father. He confesses that he is angry at her for not being there when he needed her. Following is an example of what James's prayer of repentance in relation to his mother might look like.

ᏽᎧᏨ

Jesus,

I am surprised and overwhelmed by my emotions right now. I know my mother loved me, though she didn't speak of it. She was very different from my father, but I didn't feel like she was on my side. When I remember that day in the paddock, I wondered if she watched me running. Could she tell that I was confused, angry and hurting? Why didn't she come outside? Why didn't she make sure that I was safely inside the house? I was so hungry and thirsty, afraid and confused. I felt so alone. I needed help.

But after that day, there was only silence. I could not stand that silence. Since then, I have always thought that love is weaker than fear and hate. I have not trusted my mum's love to help or support me. I resented her for not standing up to my dad, and I have promised myself that I would never become so weak. I wish she had come that night to give me a hug. For so long, I have held my mum's failure to love me against her.

Jesus, I have believed that your love is just as weak – weaker than my hurts that night and weaker than all the hurts I have carried in my life. As I remember that night, I am that lost little boy all over again, back in the paddock, needing to be rescued. These feelings tie me up in knots.

Jesus, I need you to untangle the knots of my story. Forgive me for disregarding my mum's love for me, for judging her weakness, for despising her fearfulness and for resenting her silence. Forgive me for refusing to love, because I could not bear to be like her. I am sad and angry. Please take my confusion and all my attempts to reject love. I need your help. Amen.

ॐ♋

This prayer of confession is very different from James's prayer in relation to his dad, which clearly identified his negative feelings and attitudes towards his father as well as against himself. James's feelings regarding his mother surprise and overwhelm him, and so his prayers are much softer and more tenuous. Yet he has carried resentment for his mother's 'weakness' and failure to be present when he needed her. Though he might have been just as wounded by his mother's neglect as his father's abuse, he has not been in touch with these feelings.

When James finishes this prayer of confession regarding his mother, a prayer team member prays another absolution, yet with a different tone from the previous one. This difference in tone highlights the fact that prayers in the healing ministry are not rote and mechanical, but rather situational and contextual. Each prayer needs to reflect the nuances of what is happening within the ministry setting. Following is a prayer of absolution that might be appropriate for this setting with James.

ॐ♋

Jesus,

you are gentle and full of grace, willing to receive all who come to you. As you wept over Jerusalem, you weep now over the hurt James feels around his mum. You see his tears and understand the depths of his pain and brokenness. As you walked steadily towards Jerusalem and the cross in order to face our sorrow, confusion and hurt for all time, you meet

James now, right where he needs the power of your forgiveness to comfort him and the overwhelming grace of your love to lead him to the hope of freedom and new life.

Speak to James of your tender love. Show him your wounded hands, which are stretched wide to receive him and to receive every word that he has spoken and every emotion he has felt. Enfold him in your embrace. Thank you for breaking the dark power that separates James from receiving you in truth and in love.

James, as your sister in Christ, I declare to you with deep love and confident assurance that Jesus is faithful and just to receive your confession. He is replacing it with his forgiveness and peace. He is cleansing you and taking away your confusion and hurt. It is done. Rest in the protective power of his great love for you. Amen.

ह৩ঞ৪

Other prayers of repentance

For some people, confessing a specific sin may break open a log-jam of confessions. In James's confessions about his father and mother, he also confessed his attempts at taking his own life. Because other matters may come to the surface in the healing prayer setting, it is important for members of the prayer team to resist the temptation to hurry the process. Throughout every dimension of the prayer time, we extend silent space for further reflection. The pace of healing prayer is slow and reflective.

We might also consider how James's wounding has forged certain qualities in his life over the years – both the good and shadow sides of his personality. In the book *Invitation to a Journey*, M. Robert Mulholland discusses our creation gifts[17] and then goes on to explain a more holistic spirituality.[18] In this transitional journey, he points out that 'we also need to nurture our shadow side',[19] which might include getting in touch with our wounding and recognizing the ways that it may have produced good gifts in our life. For example, James might recognize and give thanks for the way that he treats his own children very differently from the way he was treated by his father. Yet even good responses are not fully helpful if they emerge from places of reaction. Thus healing prayers are still necessary – even when we recognize that good has emerged from places of hurt.

After concluding the prayers of confession and absolution, it may be helpful to engage in a simple sacramental act. For example, James might wash his hands as a sign of cleansing, and one of the members of the team might dry his hands with a towel. These symbolic acts can solidify what is taking place spiritually and emotionally.

Conclusion

This section has focused on prayers of confession and repentance for sins of reaction against those who caused our wounding. Prayers of repentance help us begin to chart a new way forward in life. These prayers also disarm us, for they guide us to lay down our past reactions – even when we felt they were justified – because we recognize how wearying it has been to walk the road of retaliation.

Though James was deeply aware of the ways his father hurt him, James was not fully aware of the ways he had hated and rejected his father and despised his mother. When James confessed his sins of reaction against his parents, he was set free.

Thus prayers of repentance are kingdom of God prayers that stem from the heart of the gospel. Jesus proclaimed, 'The time is fulfilled, and the kingdom of God has come near; repent, and believe in the good news' (Mark 1.15). As the starting point in the journey of healing prayers, repentance sets us on the path towards a joy-filled life.

7

Prayers of forgiveness

James struggled with the idea of forgiving his father and mother for their abuse towards him and their failure in relation to his well-being, because they had already passed away long before he sought healing prayers. During the preparation time, he made it clear that this made him feel awkward – and, moreover, he did not *feel* like forgiving them. When the ministry team suggested that forgiveness was not a matter of feelings, but something the gospel calls us all to do, James expressed a willingness to forgive them during the healing ministry time.

As we saw in the last chapter, James's prayers of confession and repentance were an important first step along the healing road, and they paved the way for his prayers of forgiveness in relation to his parents, which we will discuss in this chapter.

As we will see, because James receives forgiveness from God for his own hatred and bitterness – his sins of reaction – he has been given grace for a new attitude towards his father and mother and is compelled to extend God's kindness and generosity towards them. He is also ready to forgive himself for attempting to take his own life. Through each step of the healing prayer time, God is leading James further along the pathway towards renewal and wholeness.

Introduction

In this important chapter, we clear up the confusion between confessing our own sins and forgiving the sins of others against us. Second, we provide the biblical and theological basis for the power released when we forgive others. Third, we discuss frequent problems that emerge around the issue of forgiveness. Finally, we offer several examples of prayers for extending forgiveness to others.

As we journey through this chapter, we might remember Alexander Pope's dictum: 'To err is human; to forgive, divine.' Though very complicated and often misunderstood, forgiveness has the power to release God's healing into our stories and into the world.

Confusion around forgiveness

Often, those who come for healing prayers have been shaped by contemporary culture more than they have been formed by the ethical vision of the New Testament. Our Western culture operates on a punitive justice model, where someone who has done wrong has to pay for it – typically through some form of punishment. Thus when we extend forgiveness to those who wrong us, we are resisting the trend of our entire culture.

We are also shaped by our cultural assumption that we have a right to fair treatment. If someone violates this right, then we believe that person should suffer some form of retribution. Within this model, forgiveness is not an appropriate response, because it allows perpetrators to continue to wrong others.

Having been shaped by these dominant cultural influences, those who come for healing prayers often ask, 'Why should I forgive the person who has hurt me?' Some people feel that extending forgiveness excuses the wrong behaviour, which might encourage harmful people to continue harming others in the future. Others might say, 'It is not my job to forgive' or 'I don't have the power to forgive. That's up to God.' Yet when others wrong us, we do not defend or excuse them, but we are called to forgive.

Those who have been wounded often find it particularly difficult to extend forgiveness to those who have never confessed their wrongs, apologized or asked for forgiveness. This struggle reflects the fact that in our relationship with God, we repent for our wrongdoing and then receive forgiveness. In speaking of the mission Jesus has given to the Church, Luke says that 'repentance and forgiveness of sins is to be proclaimed in his name to all nations' (Luke 24.47; Acts 5.31). In this case, forgiveness is extended on the basis of repentance – the acknowledgement of wrongdoing and turning away from such activities. Because this pattern is offered in Scripture, some feel that those who have wronged us must repent and say they are sorry before we extend forgiveness.

Yet Jesus extends forgiveness to those who never ask for it when he cries, 'Father, forgive them; for they do not know what they are doing' (Luke 23.34). Even though those who crucify Jesus do not repent when Jesus utters this prayer, he still offers forgiveness to them. Similarly, Jesus announces the forgiveness of sin when he heals the paralytic, yet the text does not indicate that the paralytic has made a confession (Mark 2.5; Luke 5.20).

With healing prayers, we are often dealing with issues that have long been buried and seemingly forgotten. Thus those who have harmed us might have moved away, disappeared or died – as in James's story. If the person who has wronged us is dead, such prayers of forgiveness in the presence of God can free us from the lifelong prison of blame and bitterness.

Yet when someone who has hurt us is still living, should we delay our own healing journeys for months or years while we wait for that person to ask for forgiveness? Clearly not! Instead, we can extend forgiveness before God, in the presence of the prayer team, and so journey further along the healing road towards freedom.

Over time, the forgiveness that we carry within us may transform those who have hurt us. Many people who have come to us for healing prayers over the years have shared stories that reflect this gradual softening of the hearts of those who wounded them. For when we forgive others in our hearts, our perspective of them changes, and this opens pathways towards mutual healing and reconciliation.

The grace of forgiveness

When we trace the large themes of the biblical story, we can see that God is very generous in the art of forgiveness. Throughout the biblical story, God's wayward people cry out for God to extend mercy to them. We see this in Psalm 79.9, among others (see also Psalm 25.18; Psalm 85.2):

Help us, O God of our salvation,
for the glory of your name;
deliver us, and forgive our sins,
for your name's sake.

This call for help is corporate and most likely takes place in a liturgical setting when the people of Israel are gathered together.

In some of the biblical narratives, one person seeks God's forgiveness on behalf of the nation. For example, Moses asks God to forgive Israel for making and worshipping the golden calf, saying that if God will not forgive the people for what they have done, then Moses will take the punishment (Exodus 32.32). Later in the biblical narrative, when the Israelites beg to return to their slavery in Egypt, Moses cries out to Yahweh: 'Forgive the iniquity of this people according to the greatness of your steadfast love' (Numbers 14.19). Similarly, at the dedication of the Temple, Solomon asks God to hear the prayers of his people when they confess their sins and to forgive them (1 Kings 8.30). In the same setting, Solomon asks God to 'forgive their sin' and also to 'heal their land' (2 Chronicles 7.14). In this same context, Solomon prays, 'if my people who are called by my name humble themselves, pray, seek my face, and turn from their wicked ways', then God will hear, forgive and heal. Clearly, the cry for forgiveness is premised on the movement of repentance. And in Jeremiah, forgiveness is sealed with this beautiful promise: 'I will forgive their iniquity, and remember their sin no more' (Jeremiah 31.34).

In the New Testament, repentance and forgiveness are at the very heart of the Christian gospel (Acts 5.31). Through Christ's redemptive work, we are no longer 'slaves of sin', but 'having been set free from sin, [we] have become slaves of righteousness' (Romans 6.17–18). John clearly spells this out in his epistle: 'If we confess our sins, he who is faithful and just will forgive us our sins and cleanse us from all unrighteousness' (1 John 1.9). After we confess our sins to God and receive forgiveness, we move towards deeper and fuller cleansing and renewal. When we do this in the presence of others, as during healing prayers, we are blessed with an absolution from our brothers and sisters, who assure us of God's generous pardon and complete cleansing.

As the happy and blessed recipients of God's generosity and grace, we can now extend that generosity and grace to others. As we have been forgiven, so we forgive, thus establishing a healing circle that ripples far beyond our personal stories.

In the New Testament, Luke emphasizes this pattern when he writes: 'Forgive, and you will be forgiven' (6.37), as well as 'forgive us our sins, for we ourselves forgive everyone indebted to us' (11.4). Similarly, Matthew writes: 'For if you forgive others their trespasses, your heavenly Father will also forgive you; but if you do not forgive others, neither will your Father forgive your trespasses' (Matthew 6.14–15). And Paul writes: 'be kind to one another, tender-hearted, forgiving one another as God in Christ has forgiven you' (Ephesians 4.32; see also Colossians 3.13). In the Gospels, we see clearly that extending forgiveness to others is neither optional nor peripheral. Thus we are not called to forgive others when we feel like it, but because the gospel demands it of us. This is the call of the gospel.

This call to obedience will always challenge us at the very core of our being, because we want to decide how we are going to respond, and we want to choose what we will or will not do. Yet, as Peter makes clear, 'once you had not received mercy, but now you have received mercy', and therefore we are called to 'follow in his steps' (1 Peter 2.10, 21). So we must humble our hearts and be attentive to what God is saying to us as we journey along the path of forgiveness towards renewal, healing and wholeness.

James's prayers of forgiveness

Now we return to the actual ministry time, when James prays to God and expresses his willingness to forgive his father and his mother for the ways that they hurt him and failed him. Before he begins, the ministry team suggests that he makes his prayers specific, rather than general. It is not enough to pray, 'I forgive my father', because James needs to give substance to his forgiveness by naming and releasing the specific details about his wounding before God. This also gives the ministry team further insights about the inner scars James has been carrying, which will guide them as the healing ministry time unfolds.

Following are two examples of prayers that James might pray to forgive his father.

ℰↃ℃ℬ

Jesus,

I have held on to these hurts for so long that I don't know who I am without them. Everything I have done and who I have become has been shaped by my relationship with my father. I don't know how to live differently, and yet I cannot continue to feed these hurts. So help me to forgive and let go. I cannot do this without your help.

Jesus, in your name, I forgive my father for being angry that day in the car. I forgive him for his difficult silence throughout that day. I forgive him for not seeing who I was during the races – but only seeing how he wished I would be. I forgive him for not cheering me on during the races, though I heard other fathers cheering on their sons.

I forgive him for never congratulating me for my grades in school. I forgive him for seeing them as worthless.

I forgive him for throwing me into the paddock. I forgive him for cursing my ability to be a good son and a real man. I forgive him for demanding that I run until I drop. I forgive him for calling me a failure. I was so frightened, angry and confused. I forgive him for this fear, anger and confusion.

Holy Spirit, please help me to remember everything I need to name and forgive . . .

I forgive my father for teaching me to see myself as a failure.

I forgive my father for not caring for me as a son that day. I forgive him for rejecting me.

In your power, Jesus, I forgive my dad for the pattern of rejection that he taught me and for how this destroyed my sense of self-worth.

I forgive him for each time that his silence and anger crushed me. I felt like he hated me. I forgive him for hating me. Jesus, I want this to end here, and so I forgive my father for hating me so much, whatever the reason. Please take from me the haunting question of why.

This is all I can think of, but if there is any other way that I can extend forgiveness to my father, I do so now, in obedience to you and in the strength of your power of life.

ॐ☯

Jesus,

you are my saviour, and I believe that because you love me, you have brought me to this time of healing. I want to obey you in offering forgiveness to my father. Please give me your power to extend forgiveness and your grace to let go.

I name to you my sadness that our relationship was not different. I wish that my father had loved me and that I had loved him back. Somehow, if this prayer can redeem what has been, please let it be so.

I forgive my father for all the tension that he brought to our relationship. I am not sure where it came from, and I wonder now if it was partly about something that might have happened to him. All I know is that as a child, I felt small, belittled, unable to please, with no understanding about how it could be different. I believed that our bad relationship was my fault, especially after that community event. I forgive my father for this tension and for its impact on me to this day.

I forgive my father for the words that he used that day: 'I will teach you to be a good son and a real man.' I suppose that being a 'good son' would have meant to make him happy or proud. I cannot recall ever seeing my father happy or proud, and I have felt my lack ever since that day. So I forgive my father for those haunting words and their impact on me to this day.

I forgive my father for dragging me to the paddock and telling me to run until I drop. I felt I was being punished, yet I didn't know why. I was confused, and my gut ached. Something happened inside me that day that hurt deeply and changed me. I have never liked myself since. I forgive my father for that punishment and its impact on me to this day.

I forgive my father for his continued silence towards me. I forgive my father for never taking down that wall of silence and for its impact on me to this day.

I forgive my father for not loving me – Jesus, help me, this hurts deeply – for not loving me, for not letting me be his son, and for the impact of that on me to this day.

For all of these things, I forgive my father and release him from the debt I have held against him and my wishing it could have been different. I give them all to you.

Now release me from the burden of unforgiveness, for your sake and for my life.

ᔕᕼᔕ

Following are two examples of prayers that James might pray to forgive his mother.

ᔕᕼᔕ

Lord,

when I think of that night, when I was running and it was getting dark, when I was afraid to stop and then could run no longer, when I stumbled and fell into the dirt on my face – my mum did not come. I lay outside in the cold darkness, and I could not move.

I was exhausted and afraid, and I was all alone on that hard ground. I felt like I would always be alone. I never thought about her absence, because I have been so focused on what happened with my dad. Her absence overwhelms me and haunts me.

Jesus, I give my mum's absence to you, and all the places where it is entangled in my story. I forgive my mum for her absence. In the moment of her absence, you have come to me as light and comfort. With your help, I release my mum from her inability to come to me that night. I forgive her for being afraid and for not standing up to my dad. I forgive her for not helping me into the house or bringing me a drink or food. I forgive her for not being there and for her silence in the days after. Lord Jesus, hear my prayer.

ᘒᘓ

Jesus,

I have chosen to follow you, and so I forgive my mum for not standing up to my father on that day. I forgive her for being silent when she could have protected me. I forgive her for not being there when I needed help to get into the house. I forgive her for not coming to see how I was or bringing me food or water. I forgive my mum for letting fear overtake her love for me and for leaving me alone that night. I forgive my mum for not being a mum that night. Jesus, I forgive my mum the way that you have forgiven me.

ᘒᘓ

Issues and implications around forgiveness

Before we extend forgiveness to those who have hurt us, we focus on their failures and hurts, and this justifies the disdain and anger we feel. As we continue to criticize them in our hearts, we reject them and try to avoid them.

But when we forgive those who have wronged us, we gradually grow into greater interior freedom as we live into a new and more spacious reality that is no longer cramped by our anger and resentment. When we forgive, we do not forget. Rather, we remember in a different way.

Though we may not tell those who hurt us about our repentance and forgiveness, over time it will begin to show. Our attitudes will become softer and more open. If we have forgiven family members, we may begin to find ways to visit them more often.

Yet our healing may require more than forgiveness. When our wounding goes deep and festers for a long time, anger and bitterness can become entrenched in our inner being, and Satan can gain footholds around our wounding. Thus we may need further prayers of deliverance and healing to guide us along the path towards wholeness and the restoration of relationships. Sometimes, this path leads to reconciliation, when those who have wronged us confess and apologize for the ways they have hurt us.

Yet such a scenario of goodness and reconciliation could not be for James, since his parents had already passed away. But over the years, James did not focus his anger and bitterness on his parents alone. Rather, those feelings spilled out and became self-destructive (through his several attempts at suicide), and they also impacted his relationships with others, particularly those who reminded him of his parents' rejection and abuse. Though James could not now live out his newfound freedom and goodness in relation to his deceased parents, he could explore new horizons in how he related with himself and others.

Those who experience wounding often struggle with underlying questions: 'Why didn't God protect me from this?' or 'If God is so powerful and caring, why didn't God prevent this from happening to me?' Some who come for healing prayers are quite 'mad' at God, because they feel that God neglected them or even abandoned them. Some might cry, 'Where were you, God, when I was raped by my uncle?' Those who are struggling with these questions may need to extend their forgiveness to God. Yet if God is the sinless one, how can we forgive him?

We must not gloss over these concerns, which touch on the mystery of God's interaction with us as we live within this fallen world. God does not put Christians into magical cocoons that protect them from all harm. For we, too, can get hurt in car accidents and storms. We, too, can lose our jobs and get sick. We, too, can get molested and abused. We all must endure the general woundedness of our world, and some people experience much more pain and difficulty than others.

Following are two prayers that might be offered when someone feels the need to extend forgiveness to God.

৪০৫৪

Lord,

I have always thought that you would protect me. But you did not when _____. At that moment, I felt that you had abandoned me. Ever since, I have felt that you failed me. So God, I want you to know that I am upset with you and angry that this has happened to me. I forgive you for failing me, and I ask you to forgive me for my anger towards you. Heal and restore me, because I want to trust you and be your friend. Amen.

৪০৫৪

Holy One,

I wish that things had happened differently. I sometimes think that you could have stopped _____. I know that Christ's victory at the cross makes a way in this broken world, and I believe that you will be faithful to complete this work. But I am suffering, and my feelings towards you have changed.

Yet Jesus suffered, too, and this comforts me. His love and forgiveness in the midst of suffering fills me with hope. Even though I do not understand suffering, and I hate pain,

I recognize that Jesus' suffering became love for me, and he asks me to do the same for others.

So I forgive you for what I do not understand. I ask you to forgive me for blaming you. Help me to suffer love and live the way that Jesus did.

80C8

Conclusion

Forgiveness is at the heart of the Christian story. For whenever we do what is wrong, we turn to God and confess our sins. Then we receive forgiveness through Christ in the blessing of the Spirit. Yet there is much more to the story of forgiveness, for others sin against us in all sorts of ways. Whether the offence is small or great, the gospel calls us to forgive those who have sinned against us.

Thus forgiveness is an essential feature in the healing journey, because it extends to others the love and generosity that God extends to us. In this way, forgiveness not only has our healing in view, but also the healing of others through the miracle of reconciliation.

Those who walk the road of confession and forgiveness experience great relief and joy, which empowers them to move further along the healing journey. L. Gregory Jones writes:

> Christian forgiveness is at once an expression of a commitment to a way of life, the cruciform life of holiness in which we seek to 'unlearn' sin and learn the ways of God, and a means of seeking reconciliation in the midst of particular sins [and] specific instances of brokenness.[1]

80C8

Dear One,

in Christ you have made a way for us to live well in the midst of a broken world, the sins of others and our own frailties. We confess that your way of forgiveness is completely opposite to how we would do things. It is difficult for us to comprehend this grace that you give.

Yet as we receive forgiveness, we live more fully. As we extend forgiveness, we become more like you. As we follow your kingdom rule, we become more and more indebted to the life you offer, and our capacity to love and forgive others grows. How peculiar, earth-shaking and life-begetting you are!

We thank you for making what seems impossible possible. Thank you for empowering us to live out your way of forgiveness. Help us to turn to you and rest in your mercy. Our hands are open to receive this gift, so that you might reconcile the whole world to yourself and us to each other. We bless your name. Amen.

8

Prayers of separation

Once James has confessed his sins and forgiven his parents for their wrongdoing towards him, most priests, pastors and lay persons would send James home. For in the modern era of the Church, the healing ministry of the faith community has been de-emphasized and outsourced to other professionals. Thus those who have medical problems go to a doctor, and those who have mental health problems or spiritual problems usually go to the psychologist or the personal therapist rather than seek healing from the Church. This is even true among Pentecostal churches in the West, which have moved away from a focus on healing towards a success-oriented gospel of self-enhancement. So even though James has made progress, we suggest that there is more work to be done. James is aware of this, since it was discussed during the preparation time.

Up to this point in the healing ministry, James has prayed many of the prayers – thus he has been fully engaged in his healing journey. He is not merely a passive recipient. Yet the prayers of separation are always prayed by the members of the ministry team.

Introduction

In this book, we call on the faith community to recover the gospel's emphasis on healing and to revitalize its spiritual formation and soul-care practices. During the pre-medieval period of the Church, those who made confession of faith were baptized, then prayed over for exorcism and the in-filling of the Spirit, and also anointed with oil for healing. Yet in contrast, many contemporary churches boil a confession of faith down to 'I love Jesus', which is followed by a handshake from the clergy and elders during a Sunday morning service. So we should not be surprised when those who enter the faith community in such an anorexic way carry unresolved issues with them. It is important for buried wounds to be uncovered and addressed at the beginning of the faith journey, rather than waiting until some crisis point.

In this chapter, we will set out the rationale for prayers of separation and offer a few examples. Though the concept of this prayer form is important, there are multiple ways to express it. As with all the prayer forms discussed in this book, readers are encouraged to craft their own variations when the language in the examples does not work for them.

Rationale for prayers of separation

Prayers of separation are concerned with our attachments. We know how important it is for children to develop positive and healthy bonding with their parents, and we also know the joy of healthy attachments through our relationships with family and in friendships. These attachments involve both volitional dimensions (when we choose to be committed to a relationship), as well as emotional and spiritual dimensions. They can also have sexual dimensions, even when the relationship is not expressed in genital sexuality. Thus our relationships go very deep.

In Scripture, we see a poignant and profound relationship of love between Jonathan and David, where 'the soul of Jonathan was bound to the soul of David, and Jonathan loved him as his own soul' (1 Samuel 18.1). This love caused Jonathan to do everything he could to defend David from his vindictive father (1 Samuel 19.1–7). This love also caused Jonathan to stand aside for David in his quest for the kingship (1 Samuel 20). Later, we read again that Jonathan loved David 'as he loved his own life' (1 Samuel 20.17).

The Johannine Gospel also speaks of a profoundly intimate bond between Jesus and his heavenly Father. Jesus 'is close to the Father's heart' (John 1.18), and 'The Father loves the Son and has placed all things in his hands' (3.35). Jesus declares, 'Everything that the Father gives me will come to me' (6.37) and, 'Father . . . I knew that you always hear me' (11.42). In teaching his followers,

Jesus says, 'If you knew me, you would know my Father also' (8.19) and 'those who love me will be loved by my Father' (14.21). He defines himself by saying, 'I live because of the Father' (6.57), 'The Father and I are one' (10.30) and 'the Father is in me and I am in the Father' (10.38; 14.11). This theme is further consolidated in Jesus' 'high priestly' prayer in John 17.

These passages reflect the deep intimacy between Jesus and the Father, but they also suggest that by faith we are invited into that intimacy. In the garden of Gethsemane, Jesus prays, 'As you, Father, are in me and I am in you, may they [the disciples and those who follow them] be in us' (John 17.21). Thus as Christians, we are invited to live in the intimacy of the Father and the Son through the Spirit.

Paul further explores this notion of bondedness within the community of faith. He declares that by faith we are bonded through baptism into Christ (Romans 6.3–4). But through the Spirit, we are also baptized into the body of Christ, the Church, in all its diversity (1 Corinthians 12.12–13). Thus the intimacy that we have with Christ is meant to flow into our relationships with the faith community. Paul then discusses how we need each other's charisms (1 Corinthians 12.14–31) and how we are to express our care and love for one another, which he describes in his pastoral letters to the churches, calling us to love one another (Galatians 5.13–15; Romans 13; 1 Thessalonians 4.9), honour one another (Romans 12.10), live in harmony with one another (Romans 12.16), no longer pass judgement on one another (Romans 14.13), welcome one another (Romans 15.7), bear one another's burdens (Galatians 6.2), be subject to one another (Ephesians 5.21), and so on. In these passages, Paul recognizes the profound attachment of the believer to Christ and therefore to the faith community.

But what happens when we experience unhealthy attachments, such as when others try to manipulate and control us, or when appropriate relational boundaries are broken? And what happens when we are wounded by our marriages or family attachments? What happens when we are abused physically, emotionally or sexually? What happens when our bonds within the community of faith harm us?

Such deep relational wounds pierce us with a double-edged sword. On the surface level, we experience the wound of neglect, abuse, betrayal, rejection, deprivation – among myriad others. But at a much deeper level, our experience of physical and emotional wounding also leaves us critically wounded spiritually. For our human relationships are symbols of our ultimate relationship with God. Thus human love is a reflection of God's love; marriage is a form of anticipation of our final bridal reality in Christ in the new heavens and earth; every friendship is symbolic of the friendship that exists in the communion of the Trinity. Put another way, horizontal wounding has vertical consequences.

When we are wounded, our reactive responses of hatred, bitterness and unforgiveness bind us in unhealthy ways to the person who hurt us. We see such unhealthy attachments when children and younger people take upon themselves the blame for an adult's abuse. These unhealthy attachments can be addressed in prayer through our faith in the liberating power of Christ.

The Bible and freedom

Although there is a psychological dimension to relational attachments, the biblical story also addresses the oppressive nature of being bound – as well as the importance of liberation. In the Gospels, we can read about being bound to the oppressive work of the evil one (Luke 13.16). And the rich young ruler was so bound to his riches that he could not respond to the call to follow Jesus (Luke 18.18–25). Moreover, the Pharisees were so bound to their religious practices and traditions that they could not hear Christ's invitation to salvation and so opposed him and sought to eliminate him (Luke 11.37–44).

Luke identifies the central ministry of Jesus as 'to let the oppressed go free' (4.18), a message of good news that harkens back to Isaiah's vision of bringing 'liberty to captives' (61.1). While some may consider liberation only in terms of freedom from sin, neither text limits freedom in this way. In Mark's Gospel, we see a much more comprehensive vision of freedom: through Christ, people are set free from oppressive spirits (1.26) and healed from various illnesses (1.31; 1.42).

The Apostle Paul also took care to proclaim the scope of God's renewing and healing activity in Christ through the power of the Spirit: 'For freedom Christ has set us free' (Galatians 5.1). Paul's emphasis here is that Christ has liberated us so that we can promote freedom – freedom from sin's domination (Romans 6.18) as well as from the powers of this present evil age (Galatians 1.4). In other words, Christ's restorative and liberating presence can be at work wherever we are bound through the brokenness and dysfunction of our relationships and our culture.

In Ephesians, Paul describes the nature of evil and brokenness in our world as 'following the course of this world' (Ephesians 2.2). Thus human wrongdoing and brokenness is shaped and influenced by the gestalt and ethos of our respective cultures.[1] While never wholly bad, our society is never wholly good either, and evil is at work through the cultural values and constructs that we might perceive as benign. For example, certain cultures elevate some people groups while marginalizing others. Such politics of exclusion diametrically oppose the gospel, where all are welcome at God's banqueting table and all are one in Christ Jesus (Galatians 3.28).[2]

But Paul's telling analysis also identifies 'the ruler of the power of the air' or 'the spirit that is now at work among those who are disobedient' (Ephesians 2.2) as a factor in human wrongdoing and brokenness. In the biblical narrative, the fallen spiritual forces at work in human affairs refer to the power of Satan (2 Corinthians 11.14) and demonic spirits (1 Timothy 4.1). Speaking of these forces, Paul writes, 'For our struggle is not against the enemies of blood and flesh, but against the rulers, against the authorities, against the cosmic powers of this present darkness' (Ephesians 6.12). Thus we are influenced negatively not only by our culture, but also by the negative spiritual forces in our world. It should not surprise us that these factors often coalesce. That is to say, cultural forces can become demonic, as we have witnessed in the twentieth century with Stalinism and Nazism.

Yet Paul's analysis goes even deeper when he speaks of us living 'in the passions of our flesh' and 'following the desires of flesh and senses' (Ephesians 2.3). Thus human sin has personal, societal and spiritual dimensions, which place us in bondage and make us 'dead through our trespasses' (Ephesians 2.5). Delivered from this complex bondage, we are 'made . . . alive together with Christ'. When we come into union with Christ through the Spirit, we are carried out of our bondage and brought into freedom, identified as sons and daughters of the living God.

Prayers of separation for James

With James, we can see how his young and sensitive inner and relational world was shattered by the emotional neglect and brutality of his parents, who never acknowledged the damage they inflicted on him. Because James could not process these wounds soon after they were inflicted, they became festering sores that defined his reality as he became a man. In this way, he became 'bound' to his parents in unhealthy and destructive ways, rather than 'attached' to them through relationships of safety, care and nurture.

Though James dealt with his unhealthy attachment to his parents by confessing his anger and bitterness towards them and then by forgiving them for their abuse and neglect, the further work of separation still needs to be done. In the next stage of his healing journey, he experiences freedom from this bondage through these prayers of separation.

In these prayers, we do not separate James from his parents, but from the harm they have done to him. Though there may have been times when his parents extended goodness to James, these have been over-shadowed by hurt, and so the hurt is the focus of prayers of separation. In praying these prayers, it can be helpful to use the image of a sword cutting through the bondage that has been caused by the wounding. Following are two examples of such prayers of separation.

&⨀Cঙ

Jesus,

thank you, that you are here not only as a friend of sinners,
but also to proclaim liberty to the captives and release to the

prisoners. Thank you for breaking the bondage that ties us to our past hurts with the power of your unchanging love that overcomes the powers of death. We bless your name.

With the sword of your Holy Spirit, we separate James from all bondage, from the negative emotions that dominated his home life: the silence, suppressed anger, and hatred. We cut these negative emotions from James and separate him from their power over him.

We name the particular day in his life when he was thrown into a paddock and made to run till he dropped as a punishment for an unfounded failure. We name this lie of failure spoken over him that has endured to this day. With the sword of your Holy Spirit, we cut from James the effects of that day and those words of failure within his body, mind, emotions and spirit.

We name the curse – that James was 'not a good son' nor 'a real man'. With the sword of your Spirit, we cut from James the effects of this curse on him as it has continued to blight him over time. Spirit of God, release James from the remembrance of this curse and replace it with the truth of your love for him.

We also name the word 'absence' and every way that this word has continued to affect how James thinks of himself and his relationships with others. We take the sword of the Spirit and cut this word and every effect of it from his life.

Now, Spirit of God, you who are the fragrance of the morning, come and speak the dawn of grace into each place where unhealthy ties have been cut and within each place of darkness that has haunted James in his relationship with his parents. Into each place of wounding, apply the sweet balm of your healing oil and bring wholeness and completion to James. Come quickly, with healing in your wings, and surround him within your warming love.

ഇൗ

Holy One,

you have made a refuge for us in Christ, who demonstrated his power through brokenness and vulnerability. Christ, by the power of this love, you have overcome everything that would separate us from you, and so we pray your love and refuge around James. Come and stand between him and all that has threatened him, bound him and stunted his ability to grow into your likeness and walk in your ways.

We declare your presence with him as he remembers that sad and stressful day when he was 13 years old – every dark emotion and place of confusion, every curse and lie spoken over him, every place of wounding that has held James captive. We place your love around him as a refuge and protection.

Against the emotional neglect and abuse of that day, we place the covering of your comfort and love. Over the many days since that day, when he has been unable to receive love from himself, others or you, we place the refuge of your love as a buffer around him.

Thank you that no lie, dark power, or evil effect can withstand the power of your light. So in every place in this story, where James remembers darkness, sadness, loss, hurt, or confusion, surround him with the light of your love. In this place of refuge, show James the blessed truth of how you see him and release him into a sweet freedom that can never be taken away.

༂༂༃

Yet for these prayers to be meaningful and relevant to those coming for healing prayers, we may need to use alternative words or images. This highlights the fact that our prayer language needs to be contextually sensitive and responsively creative. This is even more crucial when we bring the healing prayer ministry into cross-cultural contexts.

Thus prayer team members need to be attentive to the person coming for prayer and sensitive to the ever-brooding and life-giving

Spirit's guidance in order to pray beyond learned categories and forms. We are not calling for flair, but rather relevance that leads to deep inner resonance. For healing prayers to be effective, they need to use language that helps the counsellee feel at home. This is not about finding the 'right' words, but rather developing a posture that reflects God's loving and healing presence.

For example, as an alternative image to the sword, we might invite Jesus to stand between James and his parents in order to block or absorb all the wounding that has taken place. Following are two examples of such prayers.

ഇരുജ

Lord,

we recognize that James has suffered a deep wound from his parents. The roots of this wounding run deep into his story and have impacted the rest of his life. We feel the pain of this child, who received a brutal curse and punishment from his father, and who was neglected by his mother. We feel a strong grief, because this does not reflect the way that parents are meant to love and protect their children. We long for the recovery of security and safety for James.

We are also aware that James's parents might have experienced wounding earlier in their own stories. Although this does not justify the ways they wounded James, we acknowledge the truth in your word about how the sins of the fathers and mothers reach to the third and fourth generations. We humbly confess that this is part of our broken world. For if you would count our iniquities, 'who could stand, who could stand'?

But your word also promises that you will 'show mercy and steadfast love to the thousandth generation of those who turn to you'. We stand with James as he turns to you, Christ of yesterday, today and tomorrow, trusting that you will not break a bruised reed, and you will not blow out a flickering candle.

Christ of today, we place your presence and your mercy between James and all that is past. Stand between James and the wounding that he received from his parents. We ask for your saving and healing power to break and block every brokenness that has spanned the generations of James's family causing this wounding to James.

Christ of yesterday, move back through James's life and continue moving backwards through all the generations that have been touched by the brokenness of silence, neglect, curse and abuse. In every place where this wounding has caused deep loss and hurt for James – or for his parents, grandparents and beyond – establish your peace and bring healing. Like water coursing over dry, parched land, fill the cracks within this story and soften the earth, reversing the desert of these wounds and opening the pathways to new and abundant life.

Christ of tomorrow, guard James into the future, so that this wounding is stopped in its tracks for ever, from this time forth. End this unhealthy connection to the past and to this wounding by the power of your life that has overcome all powers. Let your steadfast love, healing and peace take its place and mark James in all his relationships from this day forward. We ask these things in your holy name, knowing that it will be done.

ଯ୦ଔ

Jesus,

as we have journeyed with James, many sensitive and painful moments have been exposed. We have listened to James's questions, heard his painful emotions and seen him expose the tender vulnerability of his identity, which has been misshaped by his wounding.

We feel deeply for our brother, and we share in his great sorrow. As we attend to his pain, we stand at your cross, and we too hurt. O Lord, have mercy. As we look at you on the cross, we see how you have suffered for forgiveness and love. We see how you are willing to take on the sin and brokenness of the world, including these pains that James has suffered.

Thank you that you see James's tears, and you know how the memory of that day has shattered him. You see how he has been wounded by his parents' failure to love him and provide security and comfort for him.

Thank you that through the cross and your resurrection, you mend the broken-hearted and comfort all who mourn. You were lifted up in order to draw all people to you and restore the whole world.

So in your name and by the power of your death and resurrection, we lay at your cross all the burdens that James has suffered – his hurts, questions, emotions and vulnerabilities. For all time, you absorb them into your suffering heart so that James will never have to carry them or live with them any more.

For these ashes and sorrows of his life, we receive back your oil of gladness. For the devastations of his story throughout many generations, we receive back the garland of your goodness. For every point where these hurts have marked and scarred James, we receive back your grace and the resurrection of new life.

෨෬

Even though James has dealt with his sins of reaction – his anger and bitterness towards his parents – and found the grace to forgive his parents (though long dead), he needs these prayers of separation to cut through the unhealthy bondage that attached him to his parents. Through separation prayers in the name of Christ and the work of the life-giving Spirit, those unhealthy bonds are now broken, and James can live with new freedom towards his parents and his past wounding. This new freedom is not based on denial, suppression, displacement or rationalization, but rather on the presence of the healing Christ amid the deepest places of James's wounding.

Conclusion

In this chapter on prayers of separation, we discussed how abuse causes wounds that often trap us in unhealthy bondage to those who have hurt us. Even though these wrongs may have occurred a long time ago and may not have been repeated, things will not simply right themselves over time. This is particularly true when the person who has been abused or neglected nurtures the wounding through anger, bitterness and unforgiveness and then negatively takes out those feelings on others. Such repression and displacement will never bring resolution or healing.

Healing prayers do not rake up the past in order to wallow in our hurts. Rather, we bring our unresolved hurts into the spacious presence of Christ, whose healing and transformative work stops the power of the past from thwarting and misforming the shape of our present life.

9

Prayers for deliverance

By this point, James and the prayer team have been together for close to two hours, and so it is important to ask James how he is doing. If a counsellee becomes too tired during the ministry time, it is appropriate to stop and establish a later time to continue. Since both James and the members of the prayer team are feeling fine, the ministry time continues.

Yet many Protestants and Evangelicals would argue that we have gone far enough with James, and there is no need to take the healing ministry any further. Some might suggest that there is no ministry of deliverance from evil forces or spirits, and others might say that taking the ministry any further is overkill. We disagree. In this chapter, we outline our approach for praying for deliverance with James.

Introduction

In this chapter, we will engage the most difficult and controversial dimension of the healing prayer ministry: prayers for deliverance. First, we will outline the concerns that some Christian groups have about the ministry of deliverance. Second, we will discuss themes of deliverance within the biblical narrative. Finally, we will offer suggestions about how to pray prayers of deliverance for someone like James. As we have emphasized earlier, each prayer team will need to use sensitive, contextual and appropriate language during the prayer time, particularly when praying for deliverance.

Concerns about deliverance

For a variety of reasons, Protestants and Evangelicals may halt the ministry time before prayers for deliverance are offered. Protestants who have been infected by the scholarship of liberal theologians (such as Rudolf Bultmann, quoted in Chapter 1) tend to argue that the world-view embedded in the biblical texts is ancient and, as such, should not be seen as part of the *kerygma* – the proclamation of the gospel of Christ. Thus when the Gospels speak of Jesus' ministry of casting out demons, they reflect an ancient world-view that needs to be reinterpreted through our contemporary lens. To make the gospel language relevant to our contemporary context, one might propose that Christ set people free from psychological ailments, thereby replacing the language of exorcism with the language of the counsellor. Certainly from this perspective, James does not need prayers for deliverance.

On the other hand, Evangelicals who emphasize the authority of Scripture argue that we cannot reinterpret biblical texts. Nevertheless, they may agree with many mainstream Protestants that James does not need any sort of deliverance. These Evangelicals might argue that because James has repented and extended forgiveness, he has already been set free. Others might point out that even though deliverance from oppressive spirits is evident in the mission and ministry of Jesus, it is significantly less prevalent in the Pauline Epistles. Because Paul is the founder of the early Christian faith communities, his discussion of the pastoral ministry is more relevant for the contemporary Church. This perspective would also suggest that James does not need prayers for deliverance.

Many Pentecostals, on the other hand, argue that prayers for deliverance are most appropriate, particularly during times of spiritual awakening and renewal. Within the Pentecostal movement, prayers for deliverance also play an important role within certain missional contexts, since those from primal religions often come to faith through power encounters. But some Pentecostals might not pray deliverance prayers for James, while others would make deliverance the major intervention strategy of his ministry time.

The Roman Catholic view is quite different and more complex. When coming to faith and baptism after catechesis, the candidate receives prayers that bind and throw out all the works of the evil one. Following is the explanation for this:

Since Baptism signifies liberation from sin and from its insti-
gator the devil, one or more *exorcisms* are pronounced over
the candidate. The celebrant then anoints him [her] with the
oil of catechumens, or lays hands on him [her] and he [she]
explicitly renounces Satan. Thus prepared, he [she] is able
to *confess the faith of the Church,* to which he [she] will be
'entrusted' by Baptism.[1]

If used, the traditional Anglican approach maintains a similar posi-
tion, where the candidate coming for baptism is asked, 'Do you
renounce Satan and all the spiritual forces of wickedness that rebel
against God?' To which the candidate responds, 'I renounce them.'[2]
Thus the powers of evil are negated at the beginning of one's
initiation into the Christian faith.

The Roman Catholic Church also has a special ministry of exorcism for those who are demon possessed. This rite is described as
follows:

The solemn exorcism, called 'a major exorcism,' can be per-
formed only by a priest and with the permission of the bishop.
The priest must proceed with prudence, strictly observing the
rules established by the Church. Exorcism is directed at the
expulsion of demons or to the liberation from demonic possession through the spiritual authority which Jesus has entrusted
to his Church.[3]

This rite is usually reserved for those who have been deeply involved
in occult practices, witches' covens or satanic cults. But it may also
be administered to those who have been subject to curses.

Since the Charismatic Renewal within the Roman Catholic
Church in the mid-1960s, the official ministry of exorcism has
been complemented by a more general lay ministry of prayers
for deliverance, particularly for those whose sins, woundings and
dysfunctions have become more binding and oppressive. Thus
those who hate their abusers may find that the emotion of hatred
has developed into a spirit of hatred. In this case, one's own
part in fostering hatred has to be confessed as sin, but the spirit
of hatred also needs to be cast out in the name of Jesus. Yet how

does one distinguish what is sin and what is oppression? Without clear boundaries, discernment is the only guide for knowing how to pray.

Michael Scanlan speaks to this, noting that the counsellor 'doesn't know if the basic condition is deep resentment and lack of forgiveness, deep overpowering inner wounds, or the presence of evil spirits'. He goes on to say that the healing ministry requires a 'team approach' and 'discernment to test carefully the spirits as to whether the source of the block[age] is of man or evil'.[4]

The Charismatic Renewal within the Roman Catholic Church practices the ministry of deliverance as follows: 'In the name of Jesus I bind the spirit of . . . (*name the spirit if known*) and command you to leave and to go to the place that Jesus has appointed.' As Scanlan and Cirner point out, the most basic form 'is a straightforward command to Satan and evil spirits to leave a person or a situation'.[5]

These differing views should caution us about jumping too quickly to certain conclusions about prayers for deliverance. But at the same time, we should not assume that these matters can easily be resolved. On the one hand, we do not want to give the devil too much credit by demonizing every human sin and problem. On the other hand, we do not want to eliminate the devil altogether by psychologizing everything. Clearly, these two options polarize thoughtful considerations about prayers for deliverance. Thus we need to hold together both human sinning and responsibility, along with the possibility of satanic intervention. Though this may offer a balanced perspective, we still have the difficulty of discernment.

With James, we need to discern whether or not he needs prayers of deliverance. One way forward is to ask those coming for prayer if they sense a need for deliverance prayers. Normally, this is discussed during the preparation time, as those who are seeking healing often have a sense about how deep their wounding is and whether it has produced an opening for demonic powers to gain influence in their lives. The other way forward is to rely on the spiritual discernment of members of the prayer team.

That said, during the healing prayer ministry, it is best to avoid a so-called 'power encounter', where we seek to get demonic spirits to identify themselves. First, such power confrontations may well frighten those coming for prayer. Second, some persons may be subject to autosuggestion and may say anything, whether it is true or not. Third, such an encounter may suggest to the person seeking prayer that the demonic influence is really powerful – when, in fact, this is hardly ever the case. Demonic influence, when it clusters around wounding, bitterness and unforgiveness, is never powerful when bitterness and unforgiveness have been confessed. Of course, this may be different if the counsellee has had serious occult involvement. Fourth, one can never expect demonic spirits to tell the truth during such an encounter. For Satan is called the great deceiver (Revelation 12.9), and we can hardly expect evil spirits who collude with him to reveal the truth.

The Gospels and deliverance

As with every stage in the healing journey, it is important to begin our discussion by attending to the biblical story. If healing prayers are part of the ministry of Jesus, and that ministry has been entrusted to the Church, then its major themes need to be rooted in Scripture.

Dealing with anger and bitterness and extending forgiveness to those who have hurt us are clearly part of the biblical witness, but so is the ministry of deliverance. Throughout the Gospels, Jesus sets people free from various forms of demonic oppression. In individual cases within Mark's Gospel, for example (1.23–27; 5.1–20; 9.14–29), as well as in Mark's general comment that Jesus 'cured many who were sick with various diseases, and cast out many demons; and he would not permit the demons to speak, because they knew him' (1.34), we see that this ministry was integral to the good news that Jesus came to bring.

In the above references from Mark, there is a very clear distinction between healing people of illness and setting people free from demonic oppression. In the rest of Mark's Gospel, there is no mention of Jesus casting out oppressive spirits. After Jesus heals the deaf mute (Mark 7.31–37), the blind man (8.22–26) and blind Bartimaeus (10.46–51), there are no references to an encounter with demonic forces. Furthermore, in Jesus' encounter with the rich young ruler who was bound by his riches (10.17–22), Jesus does not attempt to throw out a spirit of greed.

But to understand the contemporary ministry of deliverance within the Church, we need to recognize that Jesus entrusted this ministry to the Twelve Apostles. In a terse and unadorned comment, Mark says that Jesus 'appointed twelve, whom he named apostles, to be with him, and to be sent out to proclaim the message, and to have authority to cast out demons' (Mark 3.14). In this verse, Mark identifies proclamation and deliverance as the two core elements in the disciples' ministry. Thus it is impossible to suggest that deliverance is peripheral to the apostles' ministry.

Yet it should also be noted that Luke's Gospel broadens this mandate: 'Then Jesus called the twelve together and gave them power and authority over all demons and to cure diseases, and he sent them out to proclaim the kingdom of God and to heal' (Luke 9.1–2). Thus Luke expands the disciples' ministry to the threefold work of proclamation, healing and deliverance. He points out that this is the message and ministry that reflects the nature of the kingdom of God. The apostles act as witnesses to the in-breaking of the reign of God through the Servant King, Jesus, who came to heal sickness and push back the powers of darkness in people's lives. The Church is called to go and do likewise in the name and authority of Jesus – and so are we.

The suggestion that this unique ministry died out with the apostles makes no sense from a number of points of view. First, the coming kingdom of God will have no end until it comes to fulfilment in the age to come (Revelation 11.15; 1 Corinthians 15.24). Second, the gifts of healing were not restricted to the apostles in early Christianity, for ordinary Christians also had these gifts (1 Corinthians 12.9), and elders exercised a healing ministry (James 5.13–16). Third, in the long history of renewal movements within the life of the Church, healing and exorcisms were evident. Finally, in our time, the Pentecostal and Charismatic movements have demonstrated that this ministry is still a reality.

Unfortunately, the contemporary Evangelical movement has focused on the ministry of proclamation, while neglecting the ministries of healing and deliverance. Yet Pentecostalism has been highly adaptable and contextual and has also emphasized healing themes – and for these reasons, this movement has experienced monumental growth.[6]

Pauline perspectives on deliverance

We need to be careful that we do not overplay the differences between Jesus' and Paul's ministries. While Paul was clearly innovative in his ministry to the Gentiles, he grounded himself in the tradition of Jesus. His primary emphasis in the formation of believers within the house churches of the Pauline mission was that they should be formed in Christ. He speaks of being 'in the pain of childbirth until Christ is formed in you' (Galatians 4.19). He also speaks of his own radical identification with Christ: 'I have been crucified with Christ; and it is no longer I who live, but it is Christ who lives in me' (Galatians 2.19–20). This expression of Christo-mysticism reveals that Paul saw himself as deeply embedded in the life of Christ and in the way of Christ – and so his ministry reflects that of Jesus. This can be highlighted by the following three themes.

First, Paul also had a vision of the kingdom of God. Luke ends the book of Acts by referring to Paul's ministry of 'proclaiming the kingdom of God and teaching about the Lord Jesus Christ with all boldness and without hindrance' (Acts 28.31). Throughout his ministry, Paul speaks about the kingdom (Acts 14.22; 19.8; 28.23), and his teaching refers to the kingdom of God (Romans 14.17; 1 Corinthians 4.20; 6.10; 15.14; Ephesians 5.5; 2 Thessalonians 1.5).

Second, Paul's ministry is similar to that of Jesus. As Luke describes it, 'God did extraordinary miracles through Paul, so that when the handkerchiefs or aprons that had touched his skin were brought to the sick, their diseases left them, and the evil spirits came out of them' (Acts 19.11–12; see also 13.4–12; 14.3; 14.8–10; 16.16–18; 19.14–20). Paul himself summarizes this ministry in his speech to the Ephesian elders: 'But I do not count my life of any value to myself, if only I may finish my course and the ministry that I received from the Lord Jesus' (Acts 20.24).

Third, the Apostle Peter and the other apostles also mirror the full-orbed ministry of Jesus (Acts 3.1–9; 5.12–16), along with the non-apostle Philip, who exercises a powerful ministry of proclamation, healing and exorcism in Samaria (Acts 8.4–8).

Thus deliverance was part of both Jesus' and Paul's ministries, and it was also integral to the ministry of early Christianity – even among those who were not apostles. Clearly, this ministry was neither secondary nor temporary, and its careful recovery is necessary for the healing ministry within the contemporary Church.

Praying for deliverance with James

First, let us make it clear that James was not demon possessed. Second, the New Testament does not talk about demon possession, but uses the language 'to have a demon'. In some cases, this may refer to possession, but more often it means to be affected by or influenced by a demon. Thus we do not need to be concerned with whether a demonic entity – as a spiritual force – is *in* a person, or *around* a person or *attached to* a person or *influencing* a person. The substantive issue is that there is a spiritual influence around the wounding, and this needs to be addressed because it can cause further aggravation and deepening of the wound. Therefore, we need to pray prayers of confession as well as prayers for deliverance.

During the preparation time, James indicated that his wounding was very deep and had affected the whole of his life. He also indicated that his hatred and bitterness had penetrated his life. And he made it clear that he had made several attempts to end his life. These realities indicate the presence of powerful forces. Moreover, James indicated that he was open to prayers for deliverance, and the members of the prayer team agreed that they were necessary.

Prayers of deliverance have a particular character, for they are not addressed to God. Rather, they are commanding prayers that name what must happen. They are not addressed to James, but to the spirit(s) involved in his life. When we address these spirit(s), we are not necessarily suggesting that they are *in* his life, but they are having some influence on his life.

In a general prayer of deliverance, a member of the prayer team might say,

> In the name of Jesus, I bind every spirit at work in your life,
> and I command them to leave so that the peace of Christ
> may reign in every part of your life.

But where it is clear that a particular spirit has had an influence, or where multiple spirits are at work, then prayers of deliverance should be more specific and name the entity. In such a case, a member of the prayer team might pray,

> On the authority given to me as servant and follower of Christ,
> I bind the spirit of bitterness and command you to depart so
> that the freedom of Christ may reign in every part of his life.

Traditionally, prayers of deliverance use the language of binding and loosing. The spirit is *bound* because we are not interested in its display or manifestation, as this might distract us from the work of healing. Obviously, we don't want to display the evil spirit, but rather manifest the redemptive and restoring work of Christ. So when we bind the spirit, we prevent such a manifestation. The spirit is *loosed* because we want to break the spirit's influence on and effect in a particular person. We don't take any interest in the spirit's departure, though some suggest that when we command the spirit to leave, we should also say,

> I command you to depart to the place that Jesus has appointed
> for you.

Following are three examples of prayers that we might use in praying for deliverance for James.

৵ৎ

> Based on James's prayers of repentance and forgiveness, and
> with the authority I have been given by the Lord Jesus Christ,
> I command you, spirit of hatred and spirit of bitterness, to leave
> and never come back. You no longer have any right to be here,
> and I command you to go to the place Jesus has for you, taking

with you every effect and influence that you have had in James's life.

By the authority of the Lord Jesus Christ, I declare to you, spirit of death, that you have no right to be here. I command you to depart, along with everything you have used to hurt James and bring him to despair. Go to the place Jesus has for you and never come back.

By the power of Jesus' death and resurrection living within James, I declare to every dark spirit, named or unnamed, that your right to be here has been taken from you. Leave and go to the place Jesus has for you and never come back.

Spirit of God, breathe your healing and restoration into every place and moment that has been vacated. Blow a fresh wind of your Spirit into every corner of James's story. Bless James with a strong hope, joy and every freedom that is yours to give as you fill him with abundant life.

ଝୠ୕ଔ

James has made his choice to cling to the cross of Christ. He has renounced all dark powers and influence. And we have authority in Jesus' name that whatever we bind on earth will be bound in the spiritual realm, and whatever is loosed on earth will be loosed in the spiritual realm.

So we bind you, spirit of despair and spirit of hatred. We command you to depart and go to the place Jesus has for you. We loosen every path in James's story where you have led him to despair. We release every moment of hatred that has brought him to isolation and separation. In every one of these places, we announce the full freedom of Christ.

Spirit of lies and cursing spirit, in Jesus' name, we bind you and loosen all your influence in James's life. We silence your voice, and we announce that the herald of truth has spoken in love. We command you to leave and go now to the place Jesus has for you.

Every dark spirit that has interfered with James's life, every spirit of death that has oppressed James and tempted him to suicide, we bind you and loosen your influence over his life. We cast you out from every wound where you have wreaked havoc. In Jesus' name, leave and go now to the place Jesus has for you and never return.

Now Jesus, let the power of your blood cleanse every space, every memory, every hurt, washing away all sin and darkness, filling James with your righteousness and with your power of life. Minister your love to James and bring him the deep healing that is his because he is your child. Spirit of God, pour your comfort and peace over him like a sweet fragrance. We bless your holy name.

⬠⬡

In the beginning was life, and this life is the light for all people. The light shines in the darkness, and the darkness does not overcome it.

In the name of Jesus, we place within James the pure light of Christ's salvation. In this strong light, we command you, spirit of hatred and spirit of bitterness, spirit of death and spirit of despair, and every other spirit of the evil one to leave. You have been exposed, and you have no place in the light of Christ. We command you to take every darkness and dark influence with you. Go now to the place that Christ has prepared for you.

Spirit of God, you who brood over us and draw us near, carry the light of Christ into every corner of James's story that needs your cleansing light. Sweep out the darkness and fill every space with your release and peace. Repair every damage and restore to James what has been devoured by darkness. We declare that this is the year of the Lord's favour, and we watch you at work, with our praises rising to your throne.

⬠⬡

Conclusion

For those who are journeying towards healing, prayers for deliverance are often very difficult. Though many who have been wounded struggle to acknowledge their sins of reaction, it is often even more challenging to think about malevolent forces that might be at work in their lives. And it is never easy to come 'face to face' with those forces or entities. This is particularly true in our age, which psychologizes everything and circulates unhealthy forms of deliverance in the popular imagination (as in the film *The Exorcist*).

In this chapter, we have acknowledged different perspectives about deliverance within several church traditions. We have suggested that we cannot confine this ministry to Jesus or the early Church, since it has been carried on by the followers of Jesus. Moreover, it has been recognized by the Roman Catholic Church as well as present-day Charismatic Renewal movements. Finally, we have demonstrated how one might pray deliverance prayers for someone like James. Here again, we emphasize that these prayers are not formulas, but need to connect with each particular healing context and journey, focusing on how God is working through the Spirit. For power does not lie within us, nor in our good words or prayers, but with the healing presence of God through Christ by the power of the Spirit.

During the actual ministry time for James, we noticed that the atmosphere was lighter after we prayed for deliverance. James did not fall to the floor in the midst of a convulsion while we prayed for deliverance, but he did say that he felt relieved and that an inner pressure had dissipated. In other prayer situations, there may be more dramatic reactions, but these are a 'sideshow' and not the central plot. The central plot is to see the victory of Christ manifested in people's lives today through healing, release and relief.

৵৹য়

Heavenly Father,

we confess as your Church that we keep to the edges of your ministry of deliverance. Our culture has defined 'deliverance' as a theatrical exhibition, a power play or another form of religious oppression, and so we fear it, condemn it or pretend that we don't need it.

We forget that the liar of the world prowls like a lion, seeking to devour and to destroy. We forget that oppression is one of his trademarks throughout the whole world. We forget because we are afraid, and so we name our fears before you now.

We are afraid of losing control, and so we trust our blind, comfortable ways rather than confront our idolatries and chains. We protect ourselves with our own version of safety rather than seek the freedom you offer.

We are afraid of your deliverance, like the Israelites who wanted to go back to Egypt after the exodus. We fear that you might lead us into new and risky places. We do not want to trust you, even though you say that you will lead the blind by a path they have not known. We do not want to follow you, even though you say you will lower the mountains and raise the valleys to make the path straight.

We are afraid to step into the unknown ways of your grace, and so we bind ourselves to the hell we know and have come to expect. Though you have come to deliver us from the hand of the evil one, we have let the lies of darkness overcome your light.

We are afraid of the power of death. Because the ministry of deliverance reminds us of our fear of death, we have ignored it and have forgotten that you have overcome the prince of death.

Lord, have mercy on us and forgive us.

Holy One, these lies have become the lenses through which we see our world. We have let fear justify our choices to self-protect, rather than invite you to replace our fear with love. We can no longer hear the cries of the poor, the distressed and the stranger, and so we are not free to welcome them in Jesus' name.

Rather than protecting the dignity and sustenance of people, we choose to increase our power, inflate our hatred, justify our violence and declare our wars as righteous. We have discarded your ways of forgiveness and peace, which you established at the cross.

Our greed and striving is sucking the environment dry. We have become blind to the structures and systems that oppress our neighbours, our land and ourselves. We are weary and cannot find rest.

Lord, have mercy on us and forgive us.

O Lord, heal your Church. Deliver us from the powers and lies that bind us and hold us captive to personal, structural and national sin. Teach us your kingdom way of forgiveness and peace. Help us to renounce our personal and structural kingdoms so that you might live in us and be a light to the world through us.

Help us to turn to you when we are afraid, so that you can teach us the ways of your enduring love. Soften our hearts towards you, so that our hearts will break when your heart breaks. Humble us, so that we will use the authority you have given us to minister deliverance. Grow your compassion in us, so that we will proclaim your good news as you have called us to do. Teach us to fast and pray so that you might show us how to extend your freedom to the world. Grace us with the gift of discernment.

Holy One, renew your Church. Revive your ministry of deliverance so that we can proclaim the good news of your kingdom here on earth as it is in heaven.

Come, Lord Jesus, come, and by the power of your Holy Spirit help us to take up our cross and follow you.

10

Prayers of inner healing

———•·◆·•———

Every phase of James's healing journey contributes to his overall healing process – from his initial awareness of relational problems, to the preparation time, to his being surrounded by people who are committed to praying for him, to his sharing of his story during the actual ministry time, to his confession, to his decision to forgive his parents, to the cutting of unhealthy ties to his parents, and to the prayers for deliverance. Yet the specific prayers for inner healing gather everything together and draw it towards a fuller conclusion.

Introduction

These prayers are at the heart of healing prayer ministry. To some extent, this is the most beautiful stage of the healing prayer journey. For in these prayers, we invite Jesus – the great lover, healer and restorer – to enter the wounded places of a person's life through his life-giving Spirit. Prayers of inner healing often penetrate the wounded person most deeply and so lead him or her into the greatest joy and homecoming.

We will begin this chapter on inner-healing prayers by discussing various perspectives regarding inner healing. Second, we will reflect on the biblical perspectives that relate to inner healing. Third, we will offer suggestions about how we might pray these prayers for James. Finally, we will draw implications for the contemporary Church in exercising this ministry.

Practitioners' perspectives

No one church tradition can 'claim' the ministry of inner healing – neither the Episcopalians, nor the Roman Catholics, nor even the

Pentecostals, even though they place a great emphasis on the healing ministry of Christ for today. Though many different denominations exercise this ministry, it remains peripheral within the life of most churches. Typically, lay people who have been blessed through healing prayers take up this ministry on behalf of others in their respective churches. Even when the clergy of a particular parish bless this ministry, they seldom take it up themselves or integrate it into the pastoral ministry of the Church.

From the literature about inner healing, we can make several observations. First, it is evident that there has been no systematic theological reflection on this ministry. Second, even though there is a broad general understanding of the inner-healing ministry, there is not a common language. Third, generally speaking, the ministry has not been well grounded in Scripture. Fourth, the various perspectives have typically come from practitioners who work within their particular church tradition or minister independently from ecclesiastical oversight. Fifth, these perspectives are often packaged as particular elements, such as prayers for salvation, generational healing, prayers for physical healing, prayers for emotional healing, prayers for in-the-womb experiences, prayers for occult oppression and prayers for dealing with unholy unions.[1] When we cast the ministry of inner healing in this way, we can imply that this is *the only* way to do this ministry.

Of course, this is a danger for any book about inner healing – including this one – and so we must be careful not to view inner healing as a programmatic methodology. We must remember that the inner-healing ministry has to remain contextual and tied to the specific person's healing journey. Thus this ministry requires discernment, guidance from the Spirit and flexibility.

Though we cannot take up all of these issues here, we will address the lack of common language, since different terminology can cause confusion. To begin, many practitioners classify the healing ministry as the *healing of memories*, following Agnes Sanford's use of this phrase. Sanford first mentions 'the healing of emotions' in her initial book *The Healing Light*.[2] In her later book *The Healing Gifts of the Spirit*, she speaks of the 'healing of memories' and her vision that 'the Lord will walk back with you into the memories of the past so that they will be healed'.[3] In particular, she has in view the 'grievous memories' that we find difficult to face and forgive.[4] In her struggle to find language to describe this, she writes, 'The therapy that heals these deep wounds could be called the forgiveness of sins or it could be called the healing of memories'.[5] What needs to be clarified in this search for appropriate language is that not all healing of memories has to do with our own wrongdoing, for it is also concerned with the sins of others against us. In these cases, we are called to forgive those who have sinned against us, rather than confess our sins, although we may need to confess that we have misused the sins of others. Thus this ministry is more than simply 'the forgiveness of sins'.

Similarly, Jim Glennon speaks of praying for the healing of a memory of rejection, because the counsellee is 'joined to Christ' and 'old things have passed away' through Christ's salvific work.[6] Mark Pearson uses this same language when he suggests that homework may need to be done to bring repressed memories to the surface.[7] He also suggests that in the ministry time for healing hurtful memories, the counsellee may need to use creative imagination in visualizing what Jesus may say or do in the ministry setting.[8]

This phrase is also used in the titles of David Seamands' *Healing of Memories*, as well as in *Healing of Memories* by Dennis and Matthew Linn.[9] Both books focus on the way that memories can be suppressed and need to be brought into the light of Christ. Seamands notes that 'festering memories', which can poison a person's inner and outer life, need to be healed by Christ through the Holy Spirit.[10] This 'is not simply relief from the pain of the past . . . but a growth in Christlikeness and a maturing work of sanctification'.[11] Seamands is also concerned that we can have wrong and distorted images and memories of God that need transformation and healing.[12]

Other practitioners prefer the more common term *inner healing*. In *Inner Healing*, Michael Scanlan describes this ministry as the 'healing of the inner man [person]',[13] which seeks to bring Christ's healing to 'the [inner] wounds'[14] of a person so that he or she can receive the peace of Christ.[15] According to Francis MacNutt, inner healing seeks to address our emotional problems by bringing to light 'the things that have hurt us' and praying for the 'Lord to heal the binding effects of the hurtful incidents of the past'.[16] He continues, 'Jesus eagerly desires to show us how much he cares for us by healing us of ancient hurts that have withered or broken our hearts and spirits.'[17]

In *Deep Wounds, Deep Healing*, Charles Kraft describes this ministry using the language, 'Deep-level healing . . . [as] a form of lay counseling'.[18] He explains that this ministry 'involves prayer as a major component of the process'.[19] He summarizes deep-level healing as

> a ministry in the power of the Holy Spirit aimed at bringing healing to the whole person. Since the majority of human ailments are closely tied to damage in the emotional and spiritual areas, inner healing focuses there. It seeks to bring the power of Christ to bear on the roots from which such damage springs.[20]

To further broaden out differing perspectives, Anne White uses the language of 'deep prayer counseling' in her book *Healing Adventure*.[21] She explains: 'The purpose . . . is to lead the counsellee out of all bondages (no matter how long or with whom they have existed) into total commitment to the Lord.'[22] She continues: 'When one holds fear or bitterness, hate or self-pity for an abnormal period of time, one allows the Enemy to possess the heart and mind that should be filled with the Love of Jesus.'[23] Thus this is a ministry that brings healing from bondage through the grace of Christ in the power of the Spirit.

Yet the different language used by these various practitioners does not appear to be all that significant. For when Kraft describes deep-level healing, he also uses the terms inner healing and healing of memories.[24] Regardless of the terminology, what is clearly important is that our various forms of inner wounding – those caused by the sins of others against us, our own wrongdoing, and the harbouring of our fears and anxieties – keep us from living the abundant life that Christ seeks to bring to our lives. Whatever language we use, inner-healing prayers seek freedom, wholeness and deliverance.

Biblical perspectives

In the first chapter of this book, we outlined several biblical perspectives related to the ministry of inner healing. We won't repeat that here, but we will emphasize that inner healing is part of our full restoration in Christ. Though the biblical narratives provide specific accounts of physical healing and the ministry of exorcism or deliverance from oppressive spirits, the overall theme of the biblical story is that we are to grow into Christlikeness and Christian maturity.

The theme of Christlikeness – or the *imitatio Christi* (1 Corinthians 11.1; 1 Thessalonians 1.6; Ephesians 5.1) – is the movement of God's redemptive, or sanctifying, work in our lives, through the Spirit, as Christ grows within us and Christ's ways expand in our lives. In the language of Franciscan spirituality, we become the bearers of Christ, and we seek to extend the presence of Christ to the people we encounter and serve each day. Or, in the language of Karl Barth, we become 'little Christs', pointing to the great One, who gave his life for the salvation and healing of all.

Similarly, when we grow in Christian maturity, we grow into the fullness of life that God offers to us (Ephesians 4.13). Paul describes such maturity in his letter to the Ephesians as being grounded in the love of God and empowered to promote the well-being of the faith community. Thus maturity builds us up to bless others. Paul writes that this maturity is the 'the body's [the faith community's] growth in building itself up in love' (Ephesians 4.16).

In light of this, the inner-healing ministry is central to the work of God in our lives, for if we are to grow in maturity and Christlikeness, then we need inner renewal, and whatever is blocking God's work in our lives needs to be removed. Though our full healing will not be complete on this side of God's final future, the work of God's new creation in Christ invites us to open our inner being to the healing presence of Christ.

We open ourselves to God through confession and repentance for our own wrongdoing. But we also open to God the residual impacts of our sin, the sins of others against us and the follies of living in a broken world. Most of our wounds are internal, rather than physical – although they may have physical implications. These wounds affect us emotionally, existentially and spiritually, and so they block our growth in maturity and Christlikeness.

We may be wounded from growing up in a household with many demands and little encouragement. We may have grown up experiencing frequent relocation and little stability. We may have suffered repeated rejection, with little experience of love or welcome. We may have suffered abuse without any acknowledgement or closure. We may have been wounded by shame, fear or disappointment. Or we may have been wounded by traumatic events outside of our control, such as earthquakes, drought, floods or war.

Because all of us have been bruised by life, we are wounded creatures who walk with a limp. And so we all need to receive the good news of Christ's renewing work for our sin as well as our woundedness (Isaiah 53.4–5).

Praying inner healing for James

Along with the rest of us, James is one of God's walking wounded. Wounded by his parents' abuse and neglect, the residual effects of that unhealed wounding have been eating away at his inner life and negatively affecting his outer life. For James, inner-healing prayers will seek to bring the redemptive and healing power of Christ, through the Spirit, into the previously hidden places of his life. To face the wounds that he hoped would disappear over time, James will need courage and faith. Because time does not heal our wounds, we need to return to the untended places of wounding in our past in order to live towards recovery and wholeness.

Some may become willing to return to these places of wounding when they recognize a blockage in their present journey. Others may be stirred to return to these wounded places after a contemplative or reflective experience. For others, the willingness to go back is triggered by shame, reactive behaviours or fits of anger. However God works in our lives, we must be willing to stop and become attentive to what is going on inside of us and then open ourselves to others for discernment and prayer. And as we have seen with James, the healing journey is no quick fix. And inner-healing prayers are not a solo intervention, but part of the overall mosaic of our healing journeys.

Following are examples of the many prayers we might offer as we minister to James during this part of the healing ministry.

ঽ**অ**উ

Jesus,

we invite you into each detail of the story of James's life. Up until now, so much has been hidden, shameful and confusing. As he holds his story before you now, we pray for your healing and redemptive work. We think about this particular day when James was wounded in ways that have continued to damage him. We look to see your healing in these places.

I think of the moment when James got out of the car and was grabbed by the scruff of his neck by his father. This violent touch was meant to force and frighten James, who was only a young boy. This touch overpowered James physically and emotionally, so that he felt vulnerable and unprotected. This violent act harmed James and damaged him deeply. We name this violence and ask that you would come by your Spirit to bring your merciful touch of healing into every physical and emotional memory of that violence.

When James was dragged to the paddock and made to run till he stumbled and fell headlong into the dirt, completely exhausted, he took on a physical and emotional punishment from his father that he did not understand. Jesus, this punishment was not right. It should not have happened, and it has caused a deep wounding in James that still exists to this day. Jesus, we name this suffering to you, knowing that you have suffered with James, and we ask that you speak your strong word of truth, that this event should not have been.

Jesus, in every remembrance of the physical pain that James endured that night – his lack of breath and energy, his scraped and bruised knees, the pain he endured as he crawled into the house, up the stairs and into his room – come and apply your healing balm. Comfort him now with your fatherly love for him so that he feels safe with you by his side.

(pause)

Affirm for James that the anger he felt that night – that something was not right – was a knowing that came from you, and that in this knowing he was not alone. Thank you for being with James even in the midst of this difficult punishment. Thank you that, as James suffered, your Spirit was rising up with his spirit in protest. You agreed with his young heart. Thank you that his father's physical and emotional violence could not keep him from knowing the truth that you placed within him that night. May this be a strong light and sure refuge in his memory.

(pause)

Jesus, I think of the touch that James needed that day, which he did not receive from his father, and my heart is saddened. For all that James could have received from his father and did not, we ask that you would come and bring healing. On this difficult day, when James needed encouragement from his father – a warm touch on the shoulder, a voice cheering him on, a father's love that delighted in who he was, a kind word of affirmation that James had done his best – come and mend these memories. By your Spirit, come into each memory where James longed for and needed his father's love and care, and fill James with your tender compassion and love.

(pause)

Jesus, we ask you to mend James's emotions, particularly the anger that tells him when something is not right. Though James's anger got him through that night, the anger continued in the months and years that followed, and it began to hurt James. The anger that had been a true signal became a weapon of hatred that James used against his parents and himself. Repair James's ability to know what is not right, so that it can be a signal that leads him to seek your help. Heal his ability to attend to his emotions, so that they can do the work that you created them to do in his life – to help James and not be used against him. Heal this tender vulnerability in James.

Come, Lord Jesus, come.

ଓଓ

Father God,

though we are drawn to faith in you, we do not see you very well because our perceptions of you are twisted by our experiences with our earthly fathers. It is so confusing to be hurt by our fathers and then to assume that this hurt was somehow justified. Because we are young, we believe this lie, and so we think our hurt is wrong.

James's father told him that he failed, and James was unable to change this judgement. So James was left with a lie, and he has carried it for so long within himself that he has come to believe that you feel the same as his father. Into this lie and belief, we need you to come quickly by your Spirit to speak a new word of truth to James – that you do not see him in the same way that his father did.

Speak now the word 'delight', and let it ring in his heart like a bell, resonating out from the pain of that day and through every moment that the word 'failure' loomed over him until this prayer today. For I know that you love James, and you save him because you delight in him. May your delight towards James be a high rock, a solid ground, a foundation for each day to come.

We speak over James your unchanging love that abounds in grace, from which nothing can separate him. You are with James, whether he is in the depths or the heights, and you will never leave him. You know him, even to every hair on his head, and you love him. O Heavenly Father, hold him in your tender embrace. Set your blessing upon his head and mark for ever in his heart that he is your son. Thank you that this is your work, and you are faithful to your word.

၈�’ၷ

Holy One,

as I pray around the hurt James felt with his mum, I am aware that we are touching on what is deeply tender. A baby survives on a mother's love and care. The bond between mother and child shapes how the child comes to perceive himself or herself, others and the world.

James remembers the care that his mother gave him before this sad day, but he has never considered the impact of his mother's silence and neglect during his punishment. He knows only the confusion and pain he feels today. You have already heard his confession around his mother and the forgiveness that he has extended to her. So we need you to sort out these tender and confusing feelings, to deepen and complete the healing work that is yours to do.

I thank you that you are like a mother, that you bear us and carry us. You labour over us and watch over us even to the days when our hair turns grey. So send your labouring Spirit to mend James in his relationship with his mother. Mothering God, attend to James at each moment of that day and the next, when James needed a mother.

We name the uncomfortable silence in the car on that day. We name the silence and absence as James dragged himself into the house and went to bed hurting that night. We name the silence at breakfast the next day. The absence came from weakness and tension, and it resulted in neglect. The silence was born of fear and it resulted in neglect. We name the neglect of James's physical needs – his need for food and water, for someone to care for his cuts and bruises. We name his sense of being all alone, with no one to comfort him.

Into each of these memories, we ask for your compassion and your mothering care. By your Spirit, speak to James of your sorrow for how he was neglected. In every moment where James felt alone and isolated, send your Spirit to comfort him so that he might thrive once again.

(pause)

You know the tears that James cried that night when he was all alone in his bed. You have seen the tears that rose up in James today. They come from the same river of pain. Thank you that you treat his tears with tenderness, that you catch them and wipe them away, releasing him from the pain that caused them. Calm his spirit and hold him close to your breast as you bring healing to this river of pain and bitterness that lives in James. Transform it, as you did on the day when you made the bitter water of Mara sweet.

(pause)

In the places where fear has puffed itself up and bound James, as it bound his mother on that day, break its power and replace it with your love. Wherever fear stole courage from his mother, causing him to be alone and neglected, comfort him and strengthen him in your love. You who have gone to the depths of hell to overcome fear so that you could break this power over James, send your Spirit to minister your healing work in James.

(pause)

Scripture says that even when a mother forgets, you will never forget, nor will you ever stop loving your children. We humbly admit that we are a forgetful people, and our fears cause us to neglect what is ours to care for. For James, this hurt around his mother has caused him to believe the lie that a mother's love is weak and undependable. As James has extended forgiveness to his mother, come now and complete that forgiveness with an abundance of mothering love for James. Break the power of this lie and fill him with your protecting, nurturing love.

In the power of your Spirit, cover James with your peace. Wrap your security around him and shelter him with your love and care. Lead him further into the healing and restoration you have for him.

ℰᴑᴄℬ

We lift to you the trauma that this day had on James's schoolwork and academic hopes. We lift to you his ability to do well in school, and we see how much this wound affected his ability to study, how it distracted him and made him believe that school was worthless and that he was worthless as a student. We hear from James how his schoolwork began to go downhill. Jesus, we see with your eyes how the hurt he suffered through the behaviour of his parents bruised his capabilities and broke his perceptions of himself.

Come gently with your healing and restore what was taken away from James. For every part of this story that crushed his worth as a student, that took from him the pleasure of learning and excelling in academics, bring your comfort and healing. Grow in him once again this desire and ability, so that he loves to learn, trusts his ability to learn and will no longer be harmed by this hurt.

Give him pleasure in the good work that he is able to do, so that together you will both delight in his worthy skill.

ℰᴑᴄℬ

Jesus,

lover of our soul, we lean into your tender mercy as we move to the place of James's identity – where deep calls to deep. In this core of his being, the deep wounds that he has suffered have plagued him with ceaseless accusations, anxieties and confusions. You who set yourself towards Jerusalem to die on the cross, so that in the power of your resurrection you might

117

resurrect new life, release your healing and redeeming work in James. Overcoming One, you who yearn for us by your Spirit with groans that are too deep for words, complete your healing work in James.

Now we ask your Spirit to lift the power and truth of the cross into James's soul to shed its healing light. By the light of your living power and steadfast love, we name to you the places in James's story where he was accused and led into despair and the temptation of death.

We name the violence, neglect, silence and isolation of this hurtful day. We name his vulnerability as a child on the cusp of his teenage years – an age where his spirit was opening up to explore who he was and what that would mean in his future. We name the onslaught of accusations that sought to crush his vulnerable, sensitive spirit and take from him every joy in what he knew of himself. We name his reactions – accusations of hatred and bitterness against himself and others – that caused deep fissures in his soul and a withering of his tender spirit. We name how these things led him to the temptation of death and his suicide attempts.

You answer our cries for help by breathing your breath of life into every place that has been death to us. Right now, we breathe you in, and as your breath becomes life in our bodies, we breathe your life into our souls. Let your breath restore life to James at every moment when lies, despair and death accused him and stole life from him. Let your sweet breath chase out the stink of every accusation that he has heard, believed and held against himself and against his parents. Breathe life into every corner of his vulnerable spirit. Build up the ruins, repair the devastations and strengthen the very core of his being into fullness of life.

(pause)

Let your breath shatter the power of the shame that James has felt about not being who his dad thought he should be.

For every moment when James felt shame for not being 'athletic', replace it with your love. For every moment when he felt shame for his abilities in school, replace it with your love. For every moment when he felt shame for not being a good son, replace it with your love. For every moment when he felt shame for not being a real man, replace it with your love. For every time he believed the lie that he should have been different or better, replace all of this shame with your love.

(pause)

Through the power of your death and resurrection, may every accusation, lie, fear and anxiety that made a home in James as a result of that day be lost to him and for ever cease.

We place your cross between him and every threat of death and suicide. Strengthen the core of James's being to see clearly the lies of the evil one. Teach him to choose life over death. Strengthen and sanctify James in the truth so that he might be one with you.

Resurrect in James the joy that you have for him and the delight that you have in him. We claim the promise that through your healing work, he will know you and be known by you, and in you his joy will be made complete.

℘℃ঽ

Holy One,

in holding this story before you, James has climbed a difficult summit. As James has given his story into your care, we have had a strong sense of your presence. We settle now into your stillness and peace, sitting together at the top of this peak, looking back along the path that has led us here and towards the vista of what lies ahead. James has said he feels relief and lightness. We praise you for bringing this release and healing to James. We praise your name for this new day.

As we finish our prayers for healing, we ask that you would gather them together and complete them within your peace.

Though James's parents are gone from this world, you have the ability to finish what was left unfinished between him and them. So let your peace be a buffer of wholeness between James and his memories of his parents. Let your peace raise up any and all goodness that James shared with his parents. Release all the good memories that have been suppressed by this difficult story. Set your seal of peace upon James and upon his relationship with his father and mother and bring it to completion within your infinite heart.

As James finds himself in the secure refuge of your heart, may he rest in the deep peace and grace that you are pouring into his spirit.

ঙ৩

Conclusion

At the heart of inner-healing prayers, we invite Jesus, the great healer, to enter the places of James's wounding and bring healing and peace. We offer these inner-healing prayers in faith that Jesus, through the life-giving Spirit, is a compassionate healer who longs to bring us fullness of life.

In this chapter, we have noted the varied language used among inner-healing practitioners to describe this aspect of the healing ministry. Whatever the terminology, these prayers seek to return to the places where people have been wounded and open the spaces where these neglected wounds have had negative impacts, hampering their ability to lead full lives.

Inner-healing prayers seek to restore the broken places in our stories by inviting God's sanctifying work of redemption in our lives. Thus inner healing moves us further along our journey towards Christian maturity and Christlikeness.

11

Prayers for the infilling of the Holy Spirit

———◆•◆•◆———

Throughout every dimension of this prayer ministry to James, team members have been attending to the movement of the Holy Spirit. The sovereign Spirit is not at their command, but they look for the guidance and wisdom of the Spirit as they pray, and they watch for signs that the Spirit is present. At this point in the journey, they specifically pray for the infilling of the Holy Spirit for James.

Introduction

As we have continually emphasized throughout this book, even though the ministry of healing prayers follows a certain pattern, that pattern of prayer will need to change based on the life stories and contexts of those who are seeking prayer. Thus every dimension of the prayer ministry requires discernment.

The Holy Spirit, who is sent by the Father and the Son, brings the life and healing presence of Christ into our lives. When we pray for the infilling of the Holy Spirit, we do not attempt to force the hand of God. Rather, we seek to co-operate with God, and we pray with the assurance that God is at work in this situation.

In this chapter we will reiterate the work of the Spirit in healing prayers, explain the biblical basis for such prayers and demonstrate the practice of these prayers for James.

The Spirit in the art of healing prayers

While some people explain the things that happen to us and the choices we make as arbitrary or subject to chance, the Christian perspective is that God inhabits our very being and directs our footsteps. God works in our lives through the Holy Spirit, who gently seeks our co-operation. This life-giving Spirit draws us, rather than forces us, into the divine dance.[1]

Throughout the narrative of this book, our longing has been to see James come to fuller life in Christ. Thus we have bathed every moment of his journey with prayerful openness to the Spirit, who animates James and draws him towards the light.

We remember that the Spirit was already working in James when he made the initial move to seek help. For whenever we seek truth, help or revelation, we move towards the Spirit; and whenever we deny, avoid, hide or rationalize, we move away from the Spirit. As Jesus says, 'When the Spirit of truth comes, he will guide you into all the truth' (John 16.13).

We also recall that we were led by the Spirit as we listened to James's story and discerned how to move towards his preparation for healing prayers. As Jesus tells us, the Spirit 'will teach [us] everything' (John 14.26), and one of the gifts of the Spirit is 'discernment' (1 Corinthians 12.10). One of the great promises for the early believers was that 'all who are led by the Spirit of God are children of God' (Romans 8.14), and we may live and serve in the joy of a similar blessing.

Our encouragement to James to spend time in prayer and reflection as part of his preparation created space for him to seek the wisdom and direction of the Spirit. When we are still in the presence of God and seek God's face, the Spirit carries us into contemplation, where we become more aware of God's love for us and our need for God's grace and renewal.[2]

During the opening prayers of the actual ministry time, the team members sought both the presence and the gifts of the Spirit (Romans 12; 1 Corinthians 12). James needed the Spirit to lead him in his sharing and praying, and the team needed the Spirit's guidance in their listening, discerning and praying. They especially needed the Spirit to help them understand the roots and consequences of James's wounding, and they needed wisdom to determine the extent to which demonic spirits had gained a foothold in James's life. Finally, as we shall see, James needs the presence of the Spirit as he seeks further inner renewal and empowerment.

The Holy Spirit in the biblical story

While this is not the place for a full treatment of the doctrine of the person and work of the Holy Spirit, we do need to attend to the relationship between the Holy Spirit and this ministry. For the healing prayer ministry must be grounded within the framework of a comprehensive Trinitarian theology as well as a faith that the special workings of the Spirit did not cease in the post-apostolic era. A diminished view of the Holy Spirit will not serve us well in the art of healing prayers. Moreover, whenever we lose sight of the Spirit, we begin to rely more on our own strategies and programmes. While healing prayers have a Christological centre, they have a pneumatological outworking.

The Spirit is the gift of the Father and the Son to the faith community, who have been redeemed in Christ and sent out into the world to join God in the work of restoration. The Spirit brings the presence of God home to us, sculpts the redemptive work of Christ in us, and renews the world through movements of hope. In the simplest of terms, God is the Creator, Jesus is the redeemer, and the Spirit is the great beautifier and renewer. This kind of language is permissible, so long as we add that each person of the Trinity is wholly involved in the others' work.[3] Thus we can't think of the Father without also being attentive to the Son and the presence of the Spirit. God is a community of persons, and we are called into the intimacy of Father, Son and Holy Spirit.

A Christian is a person who 'is born of the Spirit' (John 3.8) and 'marked with the seal of the promised Holy Spirit' (Ephesians 1.13). The call of the Christian is to grow in Christ (Ephesians 4.15), and this growth is enhanced through the fruit (Galatians 5.22–23) and gifts of the Spirit (1 Corinthians 12).

In the biblical narrative, the Spirit comes to God's people in a variety of ways to lead, renew and bless. The disciples of Jesus were 'filled with the Holy Spirit' (Acts 2.4) on the day of Pentecost, and further infillings occurred again and again (Acts 4.8, 31; 9.17; 13.9). Thus the infilling of the Spirit is not a terminal experience that marks a higher stage of Christian spirituality, but rather a repeatable experience that reinvigorates, revitalizes and empowers us.

This renewal is necessary, for all too easily we move from dependence on the Spirit to self-sufficiency, from prayerfulness to complacency, from giving to emptiness. Therefore we need inner renewal continuously.

But there are also special operations of the Spirit given in specific situations. For example, in a counselling context, I may need a word of wisdom from the Spirit or the gift of discernment. We don't possess the Spirit and the Spirit's gifts as a static possession, but the Spirit gives us particular gifts within various contexts, and so we need to remain prayerful and receptive.

Praying for James

This brings us back to James and our need to pray for the infilling of the Spirit. James is a Christian, and so we are not praying for his conversion. James has received healing prayers, and so this is not a prayer for healing. James already knows the work of the Spirit in his life, and so we are not praying for a special experience of the Spirit. Instead, our prayers are specific and relevant to the art of healing prayers.

James has opened his heart, his needs and woundedness to the healing power of Christ. Our prayer for James at this point is that the Spirit will fill the places that James has brought into the open. We are asking for the comfort of the Spirit. We are asking the Holy Spirit to renew those spaces that were occupied previously with negativity, hurt and oppression. We are asking the Spirit to anoint and empower James.

☙ ❧

Spirit of God,

you pray unceasingly before the mighty throne of God, and you have helped us today. Where we did not know how to pray, you prayed in us and taught us how to pray. We have watched you move to bring healing and restoration for James. We praise the Father and the Son as you have revealed them to us today.

(pause)

Holy Spirit, it is for you to replace what the locusts have taken, the years of distance and isolation, hurt, shame and poverty of spirit. Come and renew every corner of James's being. Spring up like the dawn and empower him to live in the land of love, the kingdom of our God. Grow in him the grace to receive and offer love. Make James a testament to your power to heal and your abiding peace.

(pause)

Like the rush of clear water in a dry and thirsty land, fill every difficult day that James has experienced with your comfort and peace. Into every parched and exposed crack, refresh James with all that is good and true. Grow up in him a fruitfulness that spills into every part of his life. We lift to you every relationship that James has and those that he longs for.

We pray especially that where you have taken away his fear and distrust of love, you will strengthen his ability to move deeper into a relationship of love and covenant with another. Where you have taken away his shame and isolation, fill him with grace and companionship, so that he might receive all that you long to give him.

(pause)

Come like the fragrance of the morning that wakes us up to a new day. Fill James's spirit, emotions, body and mind with your comfort and peace. Fill James with hope for a good future that is founded on your love and grace.

Spirit, you who reveal God to us, give James the mind of Christ so that he may be filled with God's righteousness and lean into the Holy One in truth. Grow and mature James so that he might know you and the way you have for him.

(pause)

Blessed Trinity, I thank you for creating this new way in James, a path of freedom filled with your blessing and peace. Thank you that your goodness towards him will continue beyond this day because you have promised to lower the mountains, to raise

the valleys and to make straight his path. Thank you that your
hand is on his shoulder, and you will show him the way to walk.

(pause)

Gracious One, you gave James breath and you blessed him
with desires, abilities and gifts so that he can step into the good
purpose for his life with full and complete confidence. You are
pleased with him and you are glad at what you have made.
Seal him with your peace and lead him into your abundant life,
that your blessings may spill over into his circumstances, his
relationships, and his world.

We are grateful for James, for his keen observant eyes and his
ability to learn quickly. We are grateful for his humble spirit and
his eager willingness to participate in your kingdom work. We
thank you for James, and we bless you for sending him here to us.
Grant him your vision, that he might see himself as you see him
and also see the good future that you have for him.

(pause)

James, I have a picture to share with you. You are standing at
the summit of a high hill. It has been a long journey to the top.
You have worked hard to get here, and at times you have almost
given up. You were not sure if you would make it to the summit,
or why you were trying so hard, but you pressed on when your
hope was small and your strength was almost gone. Something
compelled you to keep going. It helped you and drew you to the top.

As you stand at the summit, you have a flag in your hand. As
you look at it, you begin to realize that this flag has all the
markings of your life on it – some quite dark and sombre, but
over the top of the marks of your story are bold new lines and
colours that speak of forgiveness, healing, release and peace.
Your story has been gathered into these new marks, creating a
beautiful and glorious flag.

Now you notice that Jesus is with you. His hand is on your
shoulder, and he is smiling. He is pleased and delighted with

you, and he says, 'Well done.' You recognize that he made this difficult journey with you. On the flag, your name is written in his and his name is written in yours.

As you look out across the ground you have covered, you feel the assurance of what has been accomplished. As you look ahead, a deep hope rises within you. The flag is on a mighty pole, and you lift it high into the air. With all your might, you plunge it deeply into the ground, shouting, 'Yes!' as the flag blows with the wind.

Perhaps this picture is a gift for you today. Receive as a blessing any part that affirms you or resonates with you or comforts you in God's peace.

(pause)

James, in every place that the freedom of Christ has been set into your past and into your future, we claim the power of the Holy Spirit in your life to comfort, renew and empower you just like the manna of old – all that you need for each day. And may everything that our abundant God is pleased to give you sustain you from this day forth and for ever.

‰⊃

Conclusion

In tending to the art of healing prayers, we seek the healing presence of Christ for a particular person. The Holy Spirit mediates the redemptive work of Christ – sanctification, forgiveness, healing, renewal – and makes it existentially real in a person's life. This form of healing ministry is bathed in prayer and seeks life and empowerment from the Holy Spirit. Thus we are only assistants and must look constantly to the Spirit for wisdom, guidance and enablement.

While the Spirit is at work in every dimension of a healing journey, during this portion of the ministry time, we pray that all the places that have been opened by the one seeking healing may be filled with the presence, comfort and power of the Spirit.

12

Prayers of protection and closure

Introduction

By this point, we suspect that readers will exclaim, 'My, this is a long and exhausting form of ministry!' Obviously, the art of healing prayers is not a quick-fix ministry, but a demanding one that is born out of and sustained in prayer. For this reason, it is always important to have a prayer back-up team.

Because both James and the members of the prayer team have been sustained by prayer, they are surprised by how quickly the time seems to have passed.

The focus of this ministry is to pay attention to detail and to care well for James, which brings us to the final dimensions of prayer for James in this ministry session.

In this chapter, we will highlight two additional forms of prayer. First, we offer prayers of protection for James. Second, we bring the ministry time to a close, releasing each person involved with the freedom of Christ.

Prayers of protection

Healing prayers flow out of our belief that God is with us, sustaining us and drawing near to us through the life-giving Spirit. Yet in our present-day culture, we have a rather weak sense of God's presence in the life of the Church and the affairs of society. We tend to live as if God is absent and as if we need to look after ourselves. Because of this unfortunate reality, we also do not acknowledge the presence of the evil forces that seek to bring harm to our lives.

We are not suggesting that God and Satan are equally opposed forces or that humans are mere pawns in a cosmic struggle, helplessly controlled by one or the other. God is sovereign, and the evil one is merely a subversive force, a great disturber. God's sovereignty is outworked in the redemptive suffering of Christ, who heals us and invites us to life and wholeness. By faith, through the Spirit, we embrace all that Christ offers.

Because the devil has no sovereign power, we can and should resist the force of evil. We can do this when we are safe within the love and grace of God. But because we can be tempted and led astray, we are called to be on guard and attentive – not only to the movement of the good in our lives, but also to the intrusion of evil.

In praying healing prayers, the overwhelming sense is that the ministry time is safe in the presence and protection of our gracious God. But we do touch the reality of evil during the prayer time, particularly when the evil one has gained some sort of foothold connected to the counsellee's woundedness. This can't be avoided, and so we need to deal with it appropriately.

In the light of this, our concluding prayers should offer protection for James and for everyone involved. Throughout the biblical story, God is depicted as our refuge (Psalm 7.1), our strength (Psalm 84.5) and a safe place where we can hide (Psalm 27.5). In the evocative imagery of Psalm 91, we dwell 'in the shadow of the Almighty' (v. 1), for 'under his wings [we] will find refuge' (v. 4). To pray protection over James, we might draw from this language and imagery. Following is one example of this type of prayer for James.

ᛒᏯᏣᏃ

Underneath the shadow of your wings,
we dwell underneath the shadow of your wings.
Underneath the shadow of your wings,
we dwell underneath the shadow of your wings.
Hidden close to thee,
we find rest.
Hidden close to thee,
we find rest.

(Tom Wuest)

James,

we sing this beautiful psalm and song of covering over you
and around you, and we place you in the refuge God has
for you. This refuge will be all that you need and will be
present wherever you are, today and in all your days to
come.

Holy One,

you are our comforter. You protect us from the destructive
powers of the air, from being crushed by the brokenness of
this world, and from every temptation – and so we place James
into your care and keeping. Set your mark on him as chosen
and beloved and place your wings around him as a shelter
from every disturbance of the evil one. Thank you for being
the strong, overcoming one. Hidden close to you, James is
safe from every storm that comes his way. From this day, you
are restoring him into a new way of being, a new hope for the
future, a deepening of relationship, a trust that he is not alone,
and an assurance of your delight in him. Thank you that in
you he can find rest. Bless him and keep him within your
protective care.

ഈ‍ക്ക

Other metaphors or images from the New Testament might
also be used, such as Jesus as the good shepherd. For whoever
enters into the safety of Christ, the good shepherd, 'will be saved,
and will come in and go out and find pasture' (John 10.9). This
pastoral scene depicts our wonderful freedom of movement
within the nurture and safety of Christ. Within this protective
relationship, we hear these beautiful words, 'I came that they may
life, and have it abundantly' (v. 10). Following is an example of
how this guiding image might shape a prayer of protection for
James.

ഈ‍ക്ക

Jesus,

I thank you that you are the good shepherd and that with
your shepherd's staff you go ahead of James to look for good
places of nurture and rest for him. In the days to come, provide
James with spiritual food and physical care as he settles into
the spacious goodness of this prayer time within his spirit. As
your healing work continues to reshape his emotions, mind
and will, provide a home for him within your gentle heart.

Thank you, Good Shepherd, for walking beside James and
guiding his steps into the future. Be close to him as he
discovers the path you have for him in the midst of his daily life.
Teach him to trust you and to follow your lead in his vocation,
his relationships and every new situation. Gather around him
others who follow you so that he might enjoy good fellowship
in the body of believers and a deepening friendship with you.

Thank you for walking behind James, guarding his back and
protecting him. In the darkest nights, amid every fear and
sorrow, at the onset of every disturbance and threat, remind
him that you are protecting him and watching over him. Help
him to turn to you for help wherever he feels alone or afraid.
As the good shepherd, you have given your life for your sheep,
and so we trust that you will never leave him and you will care
abundantly for him.

With you as his shepherd, James has the freedom to live well,
to be fed by you and to be protected by you. Teach him your
way and help him to grow confident in the sound of your voice,
so that he will hear you in every area of his life and be able to
distinguish your voice from the liar of this world. May he feel
safe as you hold him in your heart. May he trust you and follow
your commands.

ကလ

Another key prayer for protection comes from Ephesians 6, where
Paul speaks of the need to 'Put on the whole armour of God, so

that you may be able to stand against the wiles of the devil' (v. 11). The passage goes on to mention the belt of truth, the breastplate of righteousness, the shoes of peace, the helmet of salvation and the sword of the Spirit (vv. 11–17). This is framed by the exhortation to 'be strong in the Lord and in the strength of his power' (v. 10) and to 'pray in the Spirit at all times in every prayer and supplication' (v. 18).

This passage helps us to imagine 'dressing' James in the Lord's protection as he re-enters the fray of daily life. While inner healing in no way approximates Jesus' transfiguration narrative (Mark 9.2–8), the disciples had to come down from the mountain top and deal with a boy in desperate need (vv. 14–29). So James must be prepared to return to the issues of his daily life and the world's needs. Following is an example of a prayer for James that might emerge from this passage in Ephesians.

ℰℭ

Strong Overcoming One,

our strength is in you, so we ask that you would give James the strength of your life-giving power. Let your power permeate his memories, thoughts, hopes and desires. Empower him with your life as he moves forward today under your banner of love.

James, as fellow children of God, we place Christ's holy armour upon you so that you will be protected in every way from the evil one's distractions, distortions and attacks.

In Jesus' name, we place upon you the belt of truth, for in his truth you have everything you need to sanctify you in Christ.

In Jesus' name, we place upon you the breastplate of Christ's righteousness, so that your heart will be protected and you can grow in the knowledge of Christ and mature in your understanding of God's character and love.

In Jesus' name, we place upon your feet the ways of Christ's ever-living peace, so that wherever you walk, you may know

Christ's peace for yourself. Through your life and actions, may you become the gospel of peace to all whom you encounter.

In Jesus' name, we place in front of you the shield of faith. This faith will cover you completely and protect you from every flaming dart of the evil one, every lie and temptation that is thrown at you, every fear that would puff itself up and seek to overcome you.

In Jesus' name, we place upon your head the helmet of salvation, so that your security and assurance in Christ can never be taken from you. This helmet will protect you from discouragement during times of doubt, and it will expose and dismiss any accusations of the evil one against your frailties or anything that is unresolved. With this helmet, you can walk in the confidence of Christ's freedom and hope.

Finally, in Jesus' name, we place into your hands the sword of the Spirit, the powerful word of God. Learn of the Spirit, practise the word, and pray at all times in the Spirit, bringing before God every prayer and supplication that rises up within you. By this, you will be alert to what God is doing in you and around you, and you will remain strong and steadfast.

In this armour, stand firm and watch the glory of God and his kingdom come in your days and in the world.

Prayers of closure

While James may need ongoing support in the weeks and months to come, it is time to draw this particular ministry time to a close.

The members of the prayer time have journeyed extensively with James, who has opened his heart and revealed his brokenness to them. The team has empathized with James's suffering and longing for wholeness. By their shared bond in Christ through the Holy Spirit, they have connected with one another and God at a very deep level.

Because of the depth of this spiritual and emotional connection, before leaving the prayer time, it is appropriate to place each person into the freedom of Christ, releasing them from any spiritual or emotional bondages or difficulties. Following are examples of prayers of freedom that we might offer for all those involved.

༞༁

James,

we take this oil, a physical sign and symbol of the abundance that God has for you, and we mark your forehead with a cross. Let this cross stand within your spirit for all time to mark the life and love that is yours in Christ as it has been revealed today. May it be a strong reminder of your worthiness as you walk further into wholeness. The Lord delights in you, for you are his beloved son. Be blessed.

Spirit of God,

Gather up all the words and prayers of James's story and keep them, for you do not sleep, but will complete them as you lead James into deeper freedom. Give him a gentle space within this day and the next so that he might rest and settle into the grace that has been birthed in him.

For the prayer team that has gathered around James today and interceded for him during our prayers, I ask you to take from us what we no longer need to remember. Clear our minds and hearts and release us from the work of these hours. Cut from us any part of this prayer time that seeks to burden us and seal it within your heart.

We are so grateful to have had a share in your labour and to rejoice in your great goodness towards James. We are glad now to let go and rest, to let you continue what is yours to complete. Lord, fill us with your peace.

༞༁

To conclude the prayer ministry, a liturgical blessing might be appropriate. You might pray a benediction drawn from Scripture, such as the following one from Numbers (6.24–26).

> The Lord bless you and keep you;
> the Lord make his face to shine upon you, and be gracious to you;
> the Lord lift up his countenance upon you, and give you peace.

Or you might use the following benediction from 1 Thessalonians (5.23–24).

> May the God of peace himself sanctify you entirely; and may your spirit and soul and body be kept sound and blameless at the coming of our Lord Jesus Christ. The one who calls you is faithful and he will do this.

Conclusion

The basic movement of inner-healing prayers is for people to come into greater freedom in Christ and to grow in wholeness. Although problems are addressed during this prayer ministry, the focus is to seek the abundant life of Christ.

In this chapter we have focused on concluding prayers for protection, the empowerment of the Spirit and prayers of closure. Our overarching desire continues to be to enable James to live his life more fully in the goodness and love of God, far beyond the wounding that crippled his life for so long.

13

Follow-up and conclusion

Follow-up for James

Once James departs from this ministry time, he should not be left alone. Yet the prayer team cannot continue to carry the primary responsibility for him. During the preparation time, it is important to talk with James about pastoral involvement with his church, small group or a circle of trusted friends, as he will need to be in relationship with others who will exercise a caring and pastoral role towards him.

But someone from the team should check on James during the days following the ministry time. The point here is not so much that James should *feel* wonderfully different, but rather that he will be able to function differently. Though this may well take some time to become evident, healing is manifest when we no longer respond to life from our places of woundedness, but from the healing that is the gift of Christ.

The prayer team and others involved with James will continue praying for him after the formal ministry session has ended. Following is an example of a prayer that we might offer for James during the days, weeks and months to come.

ༀ☙ℭ

Jesus,

thank you for your faithfulness towards James and for showing us how you answered the groans of your own Spirit for him. We were so grateful to see your hand stretched out to heal.

In these coming days, we ask for your grace to continue. Stay close to James as he rests and recovers from this vulnerable time. Help him to see where the shifts you have made for him affect his thinking, choices and hopes. Give him strength and a growing confidence to trust you and follow you into a new way of being. Help him not to be afraid, but to explore the spaciousness and depths of your love towards him.

Jesus, in the confidence of our completed prayers, help James to come quickly to you with anything in his memory and spirit that needs to be remembered and resolved in healing prayer. We claim the continued ripple effect of your healing power of life in his story – back into his history and forward into his future. Develop in James a maturity and strength of spirit that is founded on a deepening trust in you. May he grow in his confidence of your transforming power as you continue to meet him in every part of his life.

We ask you to give his care group of friends and pastor the confidence and ability to make a safe place for him as he tests out new ways of living life. Give them clear eyes to see what you are doing. Help them to open their hearts towards you and him so that your Spirit might continue to bless him through their care. Grant them your discernment and knowledge and every other gift that is yours to give them as they accompany James along his journey towards wholeness.[1]

We place James within your grace, and we pray your peace upon him, this day and the next.

ಏಂಡಿ

In the following days or weeks, related issues of wounding may surface for James. This should not be surprising, as the release of heavy burdens from our memories often makes space for other matters to rise to the surface. If this occurs, one of the members of the prayer team can meet with James to pray further healing prayers.

After experiencing his own healing journey, James may want to extend this ministry to others. While James should be free to exercise this desire in whatever way possible, it is advisable for him to join in practical training with an existing ministry team, ideally within his home church.

Concluding reflections

We have carried out the ministry of healing prayers and the training of others to exercise this ministry because we believe that the redemptive work of Christ is for the whole of our being. Not only are our sins forgiven, but Christ wishes to shower his healing upon his Church and to push back the powers of darkness.

This form of healing attends to the places where we are 'stuck'. Because we can be wounded by the sins of others and also by our own wrongdoing, we can become 'stuck' in patterns of unforgiveness, hurt, anger, self-pity and inappropriate reactions to others. Clearly, this is not a good way to live, and so we are invited to face our inner struggles and 'demons' while we seek prayerfully the healing and renewing power of Christ through the Spirit.

Though we can take many pathways in the journey towards inner freedom and wholeness – including our own solo journey through reflection and prayer – this book traces the art of healing prayers and how this prayer ministry might be carried out by a team.

It is challenging to tell others about our issues, needs and struggles – particularly our sins and woundedness – because most contemporary Christians feel compelled to 'put their best foot forward' in relation to others, particularly those within the faith community. Thus few seek the ministry of inner-healing prayer.

But very likely, this says more about the state of the Church than about particular individuals. Because we no longer have a sense that we are part of a community in Christ, we tend to go to a therapist or psychologist for help rather than our brothers and sisters in the faith. This certainly does not suggest that those in these helping professions can't help us, but it does suggest that the ministry within the life of the Church has been diminished. The churches that do carry out the ministry of inner healing tend to emphasize the healing presence of Christ through the Spirit within the life of their faith community.

But generally speaking, the Church in the West has not been 'travelling' well. Because many regard it as a culturally captive church,[2] one of the greatest challenges will be to deepen its inner life. This calls for deeper attention to the theological, spiritual and missional formation of those within the faith community. In other words, it is a formation of the head, heart and hands. Although the present emphasis on formation through spiritual practices is a sign of hope,[3] a spirituality of the heart needs the support and wisdom of a theology of the mind. And both head and heart need to come to practical expression through the hands – a life of service to others.

As we think about how the Church in the West can become a more missional faith community,[4] we must consider restorative inner work for the body of Christ. For if we are going to grow into the fullness of life that Christ offers, our healing is part of our redemption. As we are healed and made whole, we begin to foster more healthy relationships and enhance growth in our communities. Though we will always remain 'wounded healers', our wellness is necessary if we are to become a healed community that can extend Christ's healing into the rest of the world.

In the lifelong journey of Christian formation, the ministry of inner healing needs to find its rightful place. For when we return to places of wounding and brokenness, Christ, through the Spirit, can bind up our wounds and pour the oil of gladness on our inner being. The following passage from Isaiah offers hope.

> The spirit of the Lord God is upon me,
>   because the Lord has anointed me;
> he has sent me to bring good news to the oppressed,
>   to bind up the broken-hearted,
> to proclaim liberty to the captives,
>   and release to the prisoners . . .
>   to comfort all who mourn . . .
>   to give them a garland instead of ashes,
> the oil of gladness instead of mourning,
>   the mantle of praise instead of a faint spirit.
>
>   (Isaiah 61.1–3)

ಶಃಬ

You who are the great I AM,

we are blessed and awed by you. Even though it is beyond our ability to comprehend your vast and complete love for us and for our world, today we try, for we have tasted your goodness, and we long for more.

Our desire grows for ourselves, for James, and for the next person that you guide into your heart. May your power of life to heal scatter grace upon grace into every corner of this world. With each taste of your goodness, multiply our hunger for your kingdom to come on earth as it is in heaven. May we understand and be faithful to you so that you can turn this world upside down into your way of peace.

Help us not to fear your power to heal, so that you can bring life into every place of death within us, the Church and this world. As we bend towards your grace, teach us how to suffer love, that you might live your way and purpose in and through us.

May the healing power of your love become the compass point within us and within every sphere of work, system and influence that we are a part of – in your Church around the world.

I hear you groan within my frail heart with such strong, deep longings that are beyond words. So pray and move in me. I allow your longing to become more than I am.

As your child, I hold hands with your dear ones around the world who also share this longing. Together, we pray, come, Lord Jesus, come.

Restoration

in my dream
we waited in shadow,
   for One said
      You would come
         and we were curious.
so we prayed Lord Jesus.

in amongst the dark
   we heard moans and
      reproachful sighs
         but we wanted to see God
so we continued.

the vulnerable groans
   deepened, widened
      we needed help
         Physician, said One
and comforted, we stayed.

strong flashes of Light
   cracked the darkness
      eyes not accustomed
         were perversely afraid
it would blind us.

did You hear we wondered
   and some left
      but everywhere was dark
         and God was faithful,
One said.

we could wait no more
   and bitterness filled us
      till One shouted,
         look!
there is light!

shocked we saw
  our hearts twisted by stone
    fears marking each face,
      dark desires in closed hands.
we saw, shocked. we saw.

now what could we say?
  what could we do?
    no darkness to cover
      no home for shame
some left, dropping honesty.

but strong Light brightened,
  warming trust grew
    to the cry mercy
      the refrain sounded Love
we were less afraid.

then Light became Fire,
  agony was bound
    pain released we were
      taken from death to life
we learned of Joy.

Fire became Manna
  in open hands
    voices grew strong
      glad Gospel drew
the curious and waiting.

then You moved through
  glass, brick, fear, death
    melting cold streets
      cresting Hope on carried cries
of a world seeking Love.

Come, Lord Jesus, come.

               (Mary Dickau)

Notes

Preface

1 For one example, see R. Cherry, *Healing Prayer* (Nashville, TN: Thomas Nelson, 2000).

1 Dimensions of the healing ministry

1 *Catechism of the Catholic Church* (Manila: ECCCE, Word & Life Publications, 1994), pp. 351–8.

2 *An Australian Prayer Book* (Sydney: The Standing Committee of the General Synod of the Church of England in Australia, 1978), pp. 568–76.

3 For example, both *The Healing Ministry in the Church* and *Christian Healing* limit discussions of healing to the New Testament. See B. Martin, *The Healing Ministry of the Church* (London: Lutterworth Press, 1960), pp. 19–28, and M. A. Pearson, *Christian Healing: A Practical and Comprehensive Guide*, 2nd edn (Grand Rapids, MI: Chosen Books, 1997), pp. 13–27.

4 M. T. Kelsey, *Healing and Christianity* (San Francisco: Harper & Row, 1973), p. 200.

5 Kelsey, *Healing and Christianity*, p. 354.

6 *Celebrating Common Prayer: A Version of the Daily Office, SSF* (London: Mowbray, 1994), p. 471.

7 Kelsey, *Healing and Christianity*, p. 209.

8 B. Heron, *Channels of Healing Prayer* (Notre Dame, IN: Ave Maria Press, 1989), pp. 22–4.

9 T. M. Finn, *Early Christian Baptism and the Catechumenate: Italy, North Africa and Egypt*, Message of the Fathers of the Church, vol. 6 (Collegeville, MN: The Liturgical Press, 1992), pp. 43–5, 218–23.

10 Kenneth Leech makes this clear in *Soul Friend: A Study of Spirituality* (London: Sheldon Press, 1977).

11 See her groundbreaking book, *The Healing Light* (Evesham: Arthur James, 1949).

12 Quoted in S. J. Grenz, *Theology for the Community of God* (Grand Rapids, MI: Eerdmans, 2000), p. 160.

13 Z. Bauman, *Postmodernity and its Discontents* (Cambridge: Polity Press, 1997), p. 96.

14 Kelsey, *Healing and Christianity*, p. 200.

15 R. Bultmann, *Faith and Understanding* (Philadelphia, PA: Fortress Press, 1987), p. 249. Author's italics.

16 Finn, *Early Christian Baptism*, p. 49.

17 See *Catechism of the Catholic Church*, p. 298.

18 See *Catechism of the Catholic Church*, p. 390.

19 For a helpful book on praying for deliverance, see F. MacNutt, *Deliverance from Evil Spirits: A Practical Manual* (Grand Rapids, MI: Chosen Books, 1995).

20 See M. Lapsley, *Redeeming the Past: My Journey from Freedom Fighter to Healer* (Maryknoll, NY: Orbis Books, 2012) and J. Steward, *From Genocide to Generosity* (Carlisle: Langham Global Library, 2015).

21 See J. Stott (ed.), *Making Christ Known: Historic Mission Documents from the Lausanne Movement, 1974–1989* (Grand Rapids, MI: Eerdmans, 1996), pp. 233–48.

22 *Celebrating Common Prayer* (readings for Thursday), pp. 110–13.

23 See C. R. Ringma, *Seek the Silences with Thomas Merton: Reflections on Identity, Community and Transformative Action* (London: SPCK, 2003), pp. 115–16.

24 A. Sanford, *Behold Your God* (St Paul, MN: Macalester Park Publishing Company, 1958), p. 178.

25 Sanford, *Behold Your God*, p. 185. Author's italics.

26 R. J. Foster, *Prayer: Finding the Heart's True Home* (New York: HarperSanFrancisco, 1992), pp. 1–4.

27 E. de Waal (ed.), *The Celtic Vision: Prayers and Blessings from the Outer Hebrides* (Petersham, MS: St Bede's Publications, 1990), p. 163.

28 Sanford, *Behold Your God*, p. 184.

29 The following books may be suggestive in exploring this theme further: S. Cassidy, *Sharing the Darkness: A Spirituality of Caring* (London: Darton, Longman & Todd, 1988); T. H. Koff, *Hospice: A Caring Community* (Cambridge, MA: Winthrop Publishers, 1980); J. Vanier, *Community and Growth* (Sydney: St Paul's Publications, 1979).

2 A case study

1 Something of that story is told in J. Grant-Thomson, *Jodie's Story: The Life of Jodie Cadman* (Homebush West, NSW: ANZEA Publishers, 1991).

3 Preparation prayers

1 A. S. White, *Healing Adventure* (Plainfield, NJ: Logos International, 1972).

2 J. Glennon, *Your Healing is Within You* (London: Hodder & Stoughton, 1978).

3 A. Sanford, *The Healing Gifts of the Spirit* (Philadelphia, PA: Trumpet Books, 1976).

4 F. MacNutt, *Healing* (Notre Dame, IN: Ave Maria Press, 1999).

5 M. Scanlan *Inner Healing* (New York: Paulist Press, 1974).

6 L. Thomas and J. Alkire, *Healing as a Parish Ministry: Mending Body, Mind, and Spirit* (Kansas City, MO: Sheed & Ward, 1992).

7 J. Wimber and K. Springer, *Power Healing* (London: Hodder & Stoughton, 1986).

8 C. H. Kraft, *Deep Wounds, Deep Healing* (Tonbridge: Sovereign World, 1994).

9 D. A. Seamands, *Healing of Memories* (Amersham: Scripture Press Foundation, 1986).

10 L. Payne, *The Healing Presence* (Westchester, IL: Crossway, 1989).

4 Inner healing: opening prayers

1 For this articulation of the whole people of God, see G. D. Fee, *Paul, the Spirit, and the People of God* (Peabody, MA: Hendrickson, 1996) and R. P. Stevens, *The Abolition of the Laity: Vocation, Work and Ministry in a Biblical Perspective* (Carlisle: Paternoster Press, 1999).

2 For this articulation, see L. M. Russell, *Church in the Round: Feminist Interpretation of the Church* (Louisville, KY: Westminster/John Knox Press, 1993).

5 Listening time: prayers of discernment

1 C. Thompson, *Anatomy of the Soul* (Carrollton, TX: Tyndale House Publishers, 2010), p. xiv.

2 See the theme of vulnerability in the formation material of Northumbria Community in *Celtic Daily Prayer* (New York: HarperOne, 2002), p. xix.

3 See J. B. Thompson (ed.), *Paul Ricoeur: Hermeneutics and the Social Sciences* (Cambridge: Cambridge University Press, 1981).

6 Prayers of confession and repentance

1 Cited by B. Martin, *Healing for You* (London: Lutterworth Press, 1965), p. 40.

2 *Catechism of the Catholic Church* (Manila: ECCCE, Word & Life Publications, 1994), p. 335.

3 *Catechism of the Catholic Church*, pp. 335–58.

4 See C. W. Gusmer, *The Ministry of Healing in the Church of England: An Ecumenical-Liturgical Study* (London: SPCK, 1974), pp. 62, 96.

5 *The Book of Common Prayer* (New York: Oxford University Press, 1990), pp. 447–8.

6 A. Sanford, *The Healing Light* (Evesham: Arthur James, 1949), p. 146.

7 Sanford, *Healing Light*, p. 143.

8 Sanford, *Healing Light*, pp. 140–2.

9 Martin, *Healing for You*, pp. 43–4.

10 D. Bonhoeffer, *Life Together* (New York: HarperSanFrancisco, 1954), p. 114.

11 Bonhoeffer, *Life Together*, p. 112.

12 Bonhoeffer, *Life Together*, p. 112.

13 D. G. Bloesch, *Essentials of Evangelical Theology*, vol. 2 (Peabody, MA: Prince Press, 1998), p. 109.

14 Bloesch, *Essentials*, p. 108.

15 Bonhoeffer, *Life Together*, p. 109.

16 Bonhoeffer, *Life Together*, p. 112.

17 M. R. Mulholland, *Invitation to a Journey: A Road Map for Spiritual Formation* (Downers Grove, IL: InterVarsity Press, 1993), pp. 49–56.

18 Mulholland, *Invitation to a Journey*, pp. 64–73.

19 Mulholland, *Invitation to a Journey*, p. 62.

7 Prayers of forgiveness

1 L. Gregory Jones, *Embodying Forgiveness: A Theological Analysis* (Grand Rapids, MI: Eerdmans, 1995), p. 230.

8 Prayers of separation

1 See J. K. A. Smith, *Desiring the Kingdom: Worship, Worldview, and Cultural Formation* (Grand Rapids, MI: Baker Academic, 2009).

2 In considering this further, the analysis of Miroslav Volf in *Exclusion and Embrace: A Theological Exploration of Identity, Otherness, and Reconciliation* (Nashville, TN: Abingdon Press, 1996), may be helpful.

9 Prayers for deliverance

1 *Catechism of the Catholic Church* (Manila: ECCCE, Word & Life Publications, 1994), p. 298 (italics in original).

2 *The Book of Common Prayer* (New York: Oxford University Press, 1990), p. 302.

3 *Catechism of the Catholic Church*, p. 390.

4 M. Scanlan, *Inner Healing* (New York: Paulist Press, 1974), pp. 36, 37.

5 M. Scanlan and R. J. Cirner, *Deliverance from Evil Spirits: A Weapon for Spiritual Warfare* (Ann Arbor, MI: Servant Books, 1980), p. 55.

6 For an articulation of this phenomenon within the Latin American context, see D. Martin, *Tongues of Fire: The Explosion of Protestantism in Latin America* (Oxford: Blackwell, 1993). For a more general discussion, see R. Shaull and W. Cesar, *Pentecostalism and the Future of the Christian Churches* (Grand Rapids, MI: Eerdmans, 2000).

10 Prayers of inner healing

1 N. Dearing, *The Healing Touch: A Guide to Healing Prayer* (Grand Rapids, MI: Chosen Books, 2002).

2 A. Sanford, *The Healing Light* (Evesham: Arthur James, 1949), pp. 129–39.

3 A. Sanford, *The Healing Gifts of the Spirit* (Philadelphia, PA: Trumpet Books, 1976), p. 109.

4 Sanford, *Healing Gifts*, p. 111.

5 Sanford, *Healing Gifts*, p. 110.

6 J. Glennon, *Your Healing is Within You* (London: Hodder & Stoughton, 1978), p. 76.

7 M. A. Pearson, *Christian Healing: A Practical and Comprehensive Guide*, 2nd edn (Grand Rapids, MI: Chosen Books, 1997), pp. 107–31.

8 Pearson, *Christian Healing*, pp. 122–5.

9 D. Linn and M. Linn, *Healing of Memories: Prayer* (New York: Paulist Press, 1984).

10 D. A. Seamands, *Healing of Memories* (Amersham: Scripture Press Foundation, 1986), p. 11.

11 Seamands, *Healing of Memories*, p. 31.

12 Seamands, *Healing of Memories*, pp. 95–122.

13 M. Scanlan, *Inner Healing* (New York: Paulist Press, 1974), p. 9.

14 Scanlan, *Inner Healing*, p. 15.

15 Scanlan, *Inner Healing*, pp. 22–3.

16 F. MacNutt, *Healing* (Notre Dame, IN: Ave Maria Press, 1999), p. 147.

17 MacNutt, *Healing*, p. 154.

18 C. H. Kraft, *Deep Wounds, Deep Healing* (Tonbridge: Sovereign World, 1994), p. 9.

19 Kraft, *Deep Wounds, Deep Healing*, p. 35.
20 Kraft, *Deep Wounds, Deep Healing*, p. 37.
21 A. S. White, *Healing Adventure* (Plainfield, NJ: Logos International, 1972), p. 117.
22 White, *Healing Adventure*, p. 118.
23 White, *Healing Adventure*, p. 124.
24 Kraft, *Deep Wounds, Deep Healing*, p. 37.

11 Prayers for the infilling of the Holy Spirit

1 See I. Alexander, *Dancing with God: Transformation through Relationship* (London: SPCK, 2007).
2 Dom Cuthbert Butler, *Western Mysticism: Augustine, Gregory and Bernard on Contemplation and the Contemplative Life* (Mineola, NY: Dover Publications, 2003).
3 See C. E. Gunton, *Father, Son and Holy Spirit: Toward a Fully Trinitarian Theology* (London: T. & T. Clark, 2003).

13 Follow-up and conclusion

1 Along with pastoral care, James may also wish to seek spiritual companioning/direction. See C. Brown, *Reflected Love: Companioning in the Way of Jesus* (Eugene, OR: Wipf & Stock, 2012).
2 L. Newbigin, *The Gospel in a Pluralist Society* (Grand Rapids, MI: Eerdmans, 1989).
3 J. P. Greenman and G. Kalantzis (eds), *Life in the Spirit: Spiritual Formation in Theological Perspective* (Downers Grove, IL: InterVarsity Press Academic, 2010) and A. A. Calhoun, *Spiritual Disciplines Handbook: Practices that Transform Us* (Downers Grove, IL: InterVarsity Press, 2005).
4 D. L. Guder (ed.), *Missional Church: A Vision for the Sending Church in North America* (Grand Rapids, MI: Eerdmans, 1998).

Bibliography

Alexander, I., *Dancing with God: Transformation through Relationship*, London: SPCK, 2007.

An Australian Prayer Book, Sydney: The Standing Committee of the General Synod of the Church of England in Australia, 1978.

Bauman, Z., *Postmodernity and its Discontents*, Cambridge: Polity Press, 1997.

Bloesch, D. G., *Essentials of Evangelical Theology*, vol. 2, Peabody, MA: Prince Press, 1998.

Bonhoeffer, D., *Life Together*, New York: HarperSanFrancisco, 1954.

Book of Common Prayer, New York: Oxford University Press, 1990.

Brown, C., *Reflected Love: Companioning in the Way of Jesus*, Eugene, OR: Wipf & Stock, 2012.

Bultmann, R., *Faith and Understanding*, Philadelphia, PA: Fortress Press, 1987.

Butler, Dom Cuthbert, *Western Mysticism: Augustine, Gregory and Bernard on Contemplation and the Contemplative Life*, Mineola, NY: Dover Publications, 2003.

Calhoun, A. A., *Spiritual Disciplines Handbook: Practices that Transform Us*, Downers Grove, IL: InterVarsity Press, 2005.

Cassidy, S., *Sharing the Darkness: A Spirituality of Caring*, London: Darton, Longman & Todd, 1988.

Catechism of the Catholic Church, Manila: ECCCE, Word & Life Publications, 1994.

Celebrating Common Prayer: A Version of the Daily Office, SSF, London: Mowbray, 1994.

Celtic Daily Prayer: From the Northumbria Community, New York: HarperOne, 2002.

Cherry, R., *Healing Prayer*, Nashville, TN: Thomas Nelson, 2000.

Dearing, N., *The Healing Touch: A Guide to Healing Prayer*, Grand Rapids, MI: Chosen Books, 2002.

de Waal, E. (ed.), *The Celtic Vision: Prayers and Blessings from the Outer Hebrides*, Petersham, MS: St Bede's Publications, 1990.

Fee, G. D., *Paul, the Spirit, and the People of God*, Peabody, MA: Hendrickson, 1996.

Finn, T. M., *Early Christian Baptism and the Catechumenate: Italy, North Africa and Egypt*, Message of the Fathers of the Church, vol. 6, Collegeville, MN: The Liturgical Press, 1992.

Foster, R. J., *Prayer: Finding the Heart's True Home*, New York: HarperSanFrancisco, 1992.

Glennon, J., *Your Healing is Within You*, London: Hodder & Stoughton, 1978.

Grant-Thomson, J., *Jodie's Story: The Life of Jodie Cadman*, Homebush West, NSW: ANZEA Publishers, 1991.

Greenman, J. P. and G. Kalantzis (eds), *Life in the Spirit: Spiritual Formation in Theological Perspective*, Downers Grove, IL: InterVarsity Press Academic, 2010.

Grenz, S. J., *Theology for the Community of God*, Grand Rapids, MI: Eerdmans, 2000.

Guder, D. L. (ed.), *Missional Church: A Vision for the Sending Church in North America*, Grand Rapids, MI: Eerdmans, 1998.

Gunton, C. E., *Father, Son and Holy Spirit: Toward a Fully Trinitarian Theology*, London: T. & T. Clark, 2003.

Gusmer, C. W., *The Ministry of Healing in the Church of England: An Ecumenical-Liturgical Study*, London: SPCK, 1974.

Heron, B., *Channels of Healing Prayer*, Notre Dame, IN: Ave Maria Press, 1989.

Jones, L. G., *Embodying Forgiveness: A Theological Analysis*, Grand Rapids, MI: Eerdmans, 1995.

Kelsey, M. T., *Healing and Christianity*, San Francisco: Harper & Row, 1973.

Koff, T. H., *Hospice: A Caring Community*, Cambridge, MA: Winthrop Publishers, 1980.

Kraft, C. H., *Deep Wounds, Deep Healing*, Tonbridge: Sovereign World, 1994.

Lapsley, M., *Redeeming the Past: My Journey from Freedom Fighter to Healer*, Maryknoll, NY: Orbis Books, 2012.

Leech, K., *Soul Friend: A Study of Spirituality*, London: Sheldon Press, 1977.

Linn, D. and M. Linn, *Healing of Memories: Prayer*, New York: Paulist Press, 1984.

MacNutt, F., *Deliverance from Evil Spirits: A Practical Manual*, Grand Rapids, MI: Chosen Books, 1995.

MacNutt, F., *Healing*, 1974, reprint, Notre Dame, IN: Ave Maria Press, 1999.

Martin, B., *Healing for You*, London: Lutterworth Press, 1965.

Martin, B., *The Healing Ministry in the Church*, London: Lutterworth Press, 1960.

Martin, D., *Tongues of Fire: The Explosion of Protestantism in Latin America*, Oxford: Blackwell, 1993.

Mulholland Jr, M. R., *Invitation to a Journey: A Road Map for Spiritual Formation*, Downers Grove, IL: InterVarsity Press, 1993.

Newbigin, L., *The Gospel in a Pluralist Society*, Grand Rapids, MI: Eerdmans, 1989.

Payne, L., *The Healing Presence*, Westchester, IL: Crossway, 1989.

Pearson, M. A., *Christian Healing: A Practical and Comprehensive Guide*, 2nd edn, Grand Rapids, MI: Chosen Books, 1997.

Ringma, C. R., *Seek the Silences with Thomas Merton: Reflections on Identity, Community and Transformative Action*, London: SPCK, 2003.

Russell, L. M., *Church in the Round: Feminist Interpretation of the Church*, Louisville, KY: Westminster/John Knox Press, 1993.

Sanford, A., *Behold Your God*, St Paul, MN: Macalester Park Publishing Company, 1958.

Sanford, A., *The Healing Gifts of the Spirit*, Philadelphia, PA: Trumpet Books, 1976.

Sanford, A., *The Healing Light*, Evesham: Arthur James, 1949.

Scanlan, M., *Inner Healing*, New York: Paulist Press, 1974.

Scanlan, M. and R. J. Cirner, *Deliverance from Evil Spirits: A Weapon for Spiritual Warfare*, Ann Arbor, MI: Servant Books, 1980.

Seamands, D. A., *Healing of Memories*, Amersham: Scripture Press Foundation, 1986.

Shaull, R. and W. Cesar, *Pentecostalism and the Future of the Christian Churches*, Grand Rapids, MI: Eerdmans, 2000.

Smith, J. K. A., *Desiring the Kingdom: Worship, Worldview, and Cultural Formation*, Grand Rapids, MI: Baker Academic, 2009.

Stevens, R. P., *The Abolition of the Laity: Vocation, Work and Ministry in a Biblical Perspective*, Carlisle: Paternoster Press, 1999.

Steward, J., *From Genocide to Generosity*, Carlisle: Langham Global Library, 2015.

Stott, J. (ed.), *Making Christ Known: Historic Mission Documents from the Lausanne Movement, 1974–1989*, Grand Rapids, MI: Eerdmans, 1996.

Thomas, L. and J. Alkire, *Healing as a Parish Ministry: Mending Body, Mind, and Spirit*, Kansas City, MO: Sheed & Ward, 1992.

Thompson, C., *Anatomy of the Soul*, Carrollton, TX: Tyndale House Publishers, 2010.

Thompson, J. B. (ed.), *Paul Ricoeur: Hermeneutics and the Social Sciences*, Cambridge: Cambridge University Press, 1981.

Vanier, J., *Community and Growth*, Sydney: St Paul's Publications, 1979.

Volf, M., *Exclusion and Embrace: A Theological Exploration of Identity, Otherness, and Reconciliation*, Nashville, TN: Abingdon Press, 1996.

White, A. S., *Healing Adventure*, Plainfield, NJ: Logos International, 1972.

Wimber, J. and K. Springer, *Power Healing*, London: Hodder & Stoughton, 1986.

Printed and bound by CPI Group (UK) Ltd, Croydon, CR0 4YY

13/04/2025

14656471-0003